MW01120326

Flower of Scotland
ROY WILLIAMSON, MY FATHER

photo: Norman Wilson

Flower of Scotland
ROY WILLIAMSON, MY FATHER

KAREN
WILLIAMSON

Gavin Browne Publishing Ltd

First published in 1993 by Balnain Books
Reprinted in 2008 by
Gavin Browne Publishing Ltd
5 Wester Broom Avenue
Edinburgh
EH12 7QU

Printed and bound in Great Britain by
Antony Rowe Ltd, Chippenham, Wiltshire
Covers printed by Wood Westworth, Merseyside

Cataloguing in Publication Data
A catalogue record for this book is available from the British Library

ISBN-10: 0-9538488-1-7
ISBN-13: 978-0-9538488-1-2
EAN 9780953848812

The Publishers would like to acknowledge all those who have given photographic material to this book — the author; Mrs V Williamson; Mrs N. Williamson; Sheena Williamson; photographers Bill Robertson, Norman Wilson and Graham Falconer and especially those photographers whose names in a very few cases remain unknown at the time of going to press. Omissions brought to our attention will be credited in future editions. The publishers would also like to thank Paddie Bell, Ronnie Browne, Sheena Williamson and Robert Williamson for their contributions to the book.

Thanks

To my dear father for being all that he was, and for never giving up on me in those darker days. I will love you always.

I am very grateful, and indebted, to Ronnie Browne, his wife Pat, and to Paddie Bell. To Ronnie and Pat for caring about my mother, my sister, and myself, during times of stress; and to Paddie because she opened her heart to let me find her memories of my Dad from the early years when they all worked together.

To my mother for her gentle guiding ways, and her strong determination to keep our family intact; and to my sister Sheena, for being human and far-sighted in her advice to me as I blundered about! To my Grandfather, for his wry look at life and humorous enthusiasm that has irked, challenged, and helped me throughout the years. To my wonderful uncle, Robert, and his family, for helping me hold together when my world seemed blown apart; and to my wee seven-year-old nephew, David, Dad's only grandson, for his wonderful matter-of-fact comments that couldn't fail to enlighten us.

I am grateful to June and Dave Sinton for the typewriter. Many thanks also to Isobel Linder, Louise Stewart, Carol Alexander, and Lorna Mitchell for their advice, and especially to Mhari Ross, who kept a watchful eye on my wild narratives! also to Sarah and Simon Fraser, for not falling about laughing at my unsuspecting ignorance when I first started to write.

To Heather McLennan, for being my shoulder-to-cry-on and a true friend indeed; to all my friends and family who have put up with me over the years, and to all my father's friends, those I know, and those that I do not. Thanks for being there for him.

Lastly: '*Thank you*' to you, the fan of The Corries. My father always spoke of his fans with respect; he told me that it was the fans who made The Corries, just as much as The Corries made the music. It was you who made him who he was, and he never forgot that. His talent for making music was inspired enormously by the acclaim from the audience.

He would smile, after a good performance, '*...The crowd was fantastic tonight!*'

Foreword

Roy Williamson and I met at the Edinburgh College of Art in 1955. Through college, athletics and rugby activities, we had what might be called a 'passing acquaintance' until, in 1959, our relationship became closer when we both moved to Moray House College of Education for art-teacher training. It was whilst there that we discovered our singing voices blended quite well into a pleasant-enough sound.

Throughout the years of The Corrie Folk Trio and Paddie Bell, The Corrie Folk Trio, and The Corries, our relationship became — especially after Roy moved north to Forres and I remained in Edinburgh — a purely business one. During all that time I found Roy to be the most private person I ever met in my life. It is with real interest then that I learn a great deal about Roy Williamson from this book, and I commend its pages to your reading.

Ronnie Browne,
August 1993

Introduction

It is a strange paradox, when writing a book about someone you knew so well, that quite often you come up against other people's views of that same person. From your safe, strong platform of secure knowledge and identity, you begin to see your subject through their eyes and experiences, too. For me, on the whole, that has been a warm and enlightening experience. Even after my father's death, each new story related to me brought a new insight into the man and a happy sense of immortality, a realisation that, in the many different memories that we have of Roy Williamson, he will never be forgotten.

You probably know all the facts and dates about The Corries, their records, who sang what, when, and where. Not so easy to discover, however, is the private, family side of Roy Williamson, a side of which he should have been proud, as we were of him. (Of course he made mistakes...he was as human as the rest of us!)

Scruffy corduroy trousers, jumpers with holes, hair that looked as though it had been through a tornado, and a tan from days of working on his boat, or fishing in the lochs and rivers; and always the humorous twinkle in his eyes, and the ready grin on his face; his tall stories and funny jokes used to have me in stitches. Yet he could command a sobering authority in public, or be plunged into stormy, silent moods, when he needed his retreat of isolation.

In writing this all too brief account, I have had to limit myself mainly to personal experiences with Dad, as father and daughter, this being the knowledge I am most qualified to relate. As a family we could not, obviously, escape 'The Corrie' side of things, nor would we have wanted to do so.

Therefore some of my own memories, as well as those of others close to Dad, may amuse and entertain you, with tales of 'tour time' as well. One or two people requested anonymity in this book and I have respected their desire for privacy. I have not written all that much about my dear sister; she has already expressed a wish one day to write her own account, and I did not want to steal her thunder.

It would have been very easy to 'gallop off at a tangent', with hundreds of stories about Dad, friends, and relatives, as well as all the people connected with the work and running of The Corries, but the book would have been enormous...and probably never finished. Therefore I have limited it to a chink of light from my own childhood with Dad, and to the tangled twists of my memory and opinions from over thirty-one years.

Hardest to find was the title. Writing the book itself was comparitively easy, the cavalcades of words flowed like a river in flood. But the title? What words could I use to describe my father's identity and genius, his nationalism and unique individual talent, and yet allow you to see the family man, the kind and caring father that only my sister and I have experienced? Eventually *'Flower of Scotland', Roy Williamson, my father* became the ideal choice. I hope he would approve.

This book is to bring you inside the family world of Roy Williamson, for ours was a life far removed from what might be imagined! I shall endeavour to give you my own view of life with my father, fame, and The Corries.

photo: Bill Robertson

photo: Norman Wilson

1

The Flower of Scotland

O, flower of Scotland
When will we see
Your like again?
That fought and died for
Your wee bit hill and glen,
And stood against him
Proud Edward's army
And sent him homeward
Tae think again.

The hills are bare now
And autumn leaves lie thick and still
O'er land that is lost now
Which those so dearly held

Those days are passed now
And in the past they must remain,
But we can still rise now
And be the nation again

words and music: Roy Williamson

The theatre rumbled and shook to the applause and roars of the crowd. The soft-hued spotlights brightened on the recently-vacated stage, and still the crowd yelled and thundered for more: *The Flower of Scotland* had worked its magic yet again.

The tone of the audience changed to cheers of delight as the two red-shirted figures strode swiftly back on stage, strumming loudly on their guitars, *'Oh, we're no awa' tae bide awa'..!'*

Their strong voices filling the theatre until every person in the seated crowd just had to join in. What a celebration, fun, what unity! The sad ballads, the working songs, jaunty reels and naughty jests...the audience joined in with them all. It was as though Roy Williamson and Ronnie Browne were leading an army, the beauty and strength of those concerts could not be echoed by anyone else.

The last line of the song rang out, '...*We'll aye cam back and see you!'*

And for twenty-nine years they had kept their promise...but this year, 1990, was different.

My father, Roy Williamson, had been diagnosed as having a brain tumour. The resulting operation was a very difficult and dangerous one, but was successful in removing 90% of the tumour. Unfortunately, in spite of every effort to stop it, it eventually grew back...with the tragic inevitable result.

People often said, "Roy Williamson? Ah yes, he's one of The Corries..."— but what did they really know about my Dad?

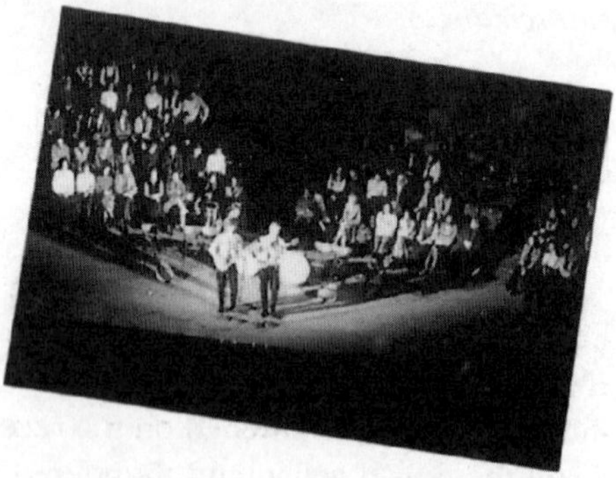

He was born on June 25th 1936 in Edinburgh, where his father was a respected advocate, who unfortunately died when Roy was only eight years old. His mother was a very elegant lady, with somewhat Victorian ideas. She was very beautiful, with interests such as drama, art and the piano — and as a girl she had done rather well in sports! It cannot be said that the relationship between my father and his mother was an easy one...it was anything but, and as the years passed she became more and more eccentric.

He spent much of his childhood and teens in Moray and Banff in Scotland—he and his brother Robert being sent to Gordonstoun School, near Elgin.

Being asthmatic is something that I, more or less, take for granted, and my father also had the affliction, as did his father before him. My grandmother however, seemed to view my father's asthma as an embarrassment, to be hidden away. Gordonstoun School was his salvation, there he enjoyed being treated as someone of worth; against all odds he consistently did well in sports, proving that asthma was no restriction to him. Many's the time he told me wonderful tales of his days at school; and yet he would not talk about his mother...it was like trying to draw blood from a stone. The hurts and horrors of his relationship with her were locked in a bricked-up cellar in his mind, and he had thrown the key where no-one would ever find it. And yet, from time to time he would accidentally open a chink in his wall around bad memories and I'd glean some information about the tall, beautiful stranger that had been my grandmother. But that was not till many years later...

My family tree is scattered with ordinary folk with adventurous tales, wide-travelled people with a love of their homeland and, here and there, gifted folk with that inherited genius or talent (that somehow passed me by!—well, there has to be a black sheep somewhere!).

We seem to have mainly originated from the Black Isle and Moray areas, although the Viking influence on our Clan Gunn roots further north had a lot to answer for. Certainly the turbulent Scots history reflected in Dad's songs could easily have been experienced by my ancestors, and was a not-so-far-away memory of real life. Thomas Macrae, for example, had a young son Alexander Macrae, born in 1734, and this lad was there in the drizzle and gloom of that horrific, dark day at Culloden in 1746. How he must have stood wide-eyed and awestruck, perhaps with a tremble of fear at the loud fire of the guns or the pained screams of the wounded men. Horses whinnying and plunging, claymores and bayonets scarlet and flashing.

Alexander would have witnessed the battle as a young lad of twelve, but, from his hiding place, little did he realise that in the far distant future—one completely beyond his ken, when people would fly through the skies to other (in *his* time unexplored) countries—or speak to each other in minutes on a telephone no matter how far apart—where other nations' wars could be re-lived through a box in each home called a television—little did he realise that the story of this last great battle on Scottish soil would still be told in the age-old way of song and legend, and that his own great-great-great-great-grandson would be one of the most popular minstrels to do this.

And Alexander's grand-daughter Isobel bravely sailed the treacherous seas in 1799 to North America; it would have seemed an even larger country in those days, hostile, rough, rugged and yet beautiful, and every day unpredictable and uncertain.

But the pioneering spirit runs strongly in the family, my father, too, loved risk and adventures, and to live a little on the narrow, sharp edge of life; hence his early involvement with the Outward Bound School and his love of mountains and the sea.

Sometimes I wish we had telephones that didn't just span

countries, but could dial back in time, so that I could tell Alexander Macrae that his blood goes on; Culloden will never be forgotten; and that he would have been proud of his great-great-great-great-grandson Roy, and that I could play over that long-distance crackling line the songs and ballads The Corries made famous, to all the folk that made us, and hear back what they'd have to say.

Trying to glean information about the Williamson family tree was difficult. Dad wouldn't talk much about his mother and father, nor about his grandparents. However with his love of history and inspired imagination he often delved further back.

I do remember how on one such occasion he told me about the Vikings. It was late at night, a wind had picked up in the darkness of the trees outside, occasionally moaning through the draughts in my cottage. The log fire was well ablaze in the hearth of the sitting room illuminated by its dancing flames. Shadows cavorted and leapt along the walls, and Dad's eyes twinkled as he cast his mind back to tales of long before our lifetimes. I just wish he could have told you this story in his own words and with his 'tongue-in-cheek' humour, he'd have done a far better job than I can, as anyone who knew him well will remember!

"There were three longships," he began, (and instantly my mind had the picture of their creaking timbers and huge striped sails billowing in the strong sea-wind).

"...The weather was hard on the Norsemen; great waves rolled and broke, water cascading into the Viking crafts, huge grey walls of water with enormous strength and stinging swirls of heavy salt spray —"

"—Where had they come from, Dad?"

"—They were three ships sent to invade Britain with a larger fleet commanded by the great leader, Ragnar Hairy Breeks!..."

(Dad gave that half-grin and quizzical twitch of the eyebrows that indicated humour!)

A Viking longship, drawn by 13 year-old Roy

"...He was called 'Ragnar Hairy Breeks' because he always wore furry trousers..."

"— Not much of a name for a great warrior and leader," I commented.

"—Well, if you think about it, Karen, all our names have specific meanings. The name William had Viking origins in our case and, somewhere along the line, came the son of William, hence Williamson."

It was quite true. I thought about other surnames, and how 'Mac' was Scots for son, hence MacRae, the son of Rae, and there were people called after their occupations like Coupar or Fisher, add to that dialect and spelling and some names change quite a bit from their original meaning.

"...The boats were in a bad way, taking on water fast," Dad went on, and again I was transported by his words to hear the howl of the wind and roar of the water smashing on the shuddering wooden frames. In my mind's eye I could see the sails ripped and tattered and hear strong Norse voices shouting in words I couldn't understand.

"Landfall was in sight, and at last the boats hove-to and rasped up onto the sand and shingle of a beach..."

"...What happened next, Dad, did they starve? where did

they land exactly?"

He smiled in the red glow of the fire, took a gulp of coffee and lit up a cigarette. Always a master of suspense he knew just when to keep you waiting....it could be infuriating at times!

"...There were some peasants walking along the beach, local Scots people, for the boats had come ashore at Caithness on the east coast of northern Scotland..."

My imagination rocketed off, putting pictures to the words he related. But somehow things then took on a Monty Python type of humour; I could 'see' a group of old crones—great baskets strapped to their backs, shawls round stooped shoulders—amazed to see these tall, fiery warriors armed to the teeth and looking for battle, walking along 'their' stretch of beach. I could imagine the gossip and the 'Well, well, well, what is the world coming to?' remarks. The Vikings also must have been surprised as well as quite disorientated. I wondered how they met—even worse, they couldn't speak each other's language, so communication must have been pretty interesting, to put it mildly. Dad continued,

"A meeting was held between the local members of the Clan Gunn and the somewhat unnerved agressors. It was obvious that the Vikings could not go home, their ships were almost wrecked, besides they had the Glory of all Norsemen (and their leader, Ragnar Hairy Breeks) to defend. So through exasperated miming, drawing in the sand, and grunting, it was explained to the Clan Gunn that they had two options: they could give the Vikings some land to farm and the right to fish, and welcome them into their community, or they could be raped, pillaged and murdered and their community taken over..."

"...What did they do? "

He gulped down some more coffee and went on,

"—Well, the canny Scots, they agreed to the Vikings' requests—and even gave them the bit of land with the nice view of the sea, right next to the beach!"

I was disappointed, somehow I had felt sure there would have been a battle.

"...Ah, but that wasn't the end of it;"

"—No?"

"...You know Scots humour: the Gunns had the last word, because the land they gave the Vikings was nothing but a shade of salt-laden topsoil—with the rest all sand!! They must have had a laugh watching the Vikings trying to grow crops in that!"

I grinned, it was a typical Scottish jest. The humour always there even in the face of danger!

"Did the Vikings starve to death? No, they saw through the trick eventually, and again issued threats to the Gunns, but this time with a little less spirit, and after a while they integrated with the Gunns and became part of our family tree—"

"—Wow, quite a noble family tree!" I remarked.

"—Along with all the tinkers, travellers and horse thieves that we became well known for in later years!"

("So *that's* where I get my love of horses," I teased.)

Roy's father, Archibald Williamson

I'm not sure how Dad found this story about the Vikings, or even if it is the truth, but I believed it. I loved to listen to his stories, he had a talent for bringing such tales to life.

There were farmers, doctors and a large number of ministers in our family way back. There were also teachers, and that 'learning' continued for a short while in both Dad and me.

My father's grandfather, Robert Moir Williamson, was born at Duffus, near Elgin, in 1867, the son of George Williamson and Elspet Morrison, farming people. Robert met Katherine Hogg and they were married in 1896. They had a son, my grandfather, by the name of Archibald Moir Macrae Williamson, born in Aberdeen in 1899, a man I wish I could have met and learned from. He became a lawyer and advocate in Edinburgh, much respected, and although he died young in 1944, he is still held in high esteem by lawyers in Edinburgh today.

Agnes Ethel Stewart Cumming, my father's mother, was

Roy's mother

born in Haddington on the outskirts of Edinburgh, in 1903, a daughter of John and Ann (Buchanan) Cumming. I have a photo of Dad's mother taken at her wedding with Archibald. She looks so pretty and slim, with a beautiful white silk wedding dress and a flowing, white silk train in a long, elegant swirl behind her.

Robert, my kind and helpful uncle, was born in 1935, and my father, Roy Murdoch Buchanan Williamson, (or as people used to tease him, 'R.M.B.W.'), came along in 1936, in Edinburgh, the same birth place as his elder brother. But for Dad his true home was always in the North and, like the salmon he used to fish, time and again his 'roots' and the call of his ancestors lured him back to Duffus and Gordonstoun, where he grew up.

2

I asked my uncle Robert if he had any childhood memories about my father, from the time when they were very small. Robert frowned thoughtfully, casting his mind back down the well-travelled path of life experience to its early beginnings; it was hard for him to remember anything specific at first.

But snatches of half-recalled images surfaced, disjointedly and out of sequence in time. Fond memories that made him smile, others that left him puzzled, or sad. Sometimes he wished that he could ask Dad questions about those long-ago days, remembering ruefully that Dad couldn't answer now. But then, like flood-gates opening, happier memories came surging in startling clarity.

For their early schooling, both Roy and Robert were sent to a Rudolph Steiner school in Edinburgh, but were evacuated to the Borders soon after the outbreak of war. Just under a year later their parents decided that the boys should return to Edinburgh and attend the Edinburgh Academy Primary School, the reason being that bombing was a lesser risk compared to the disadvantages of the children being sent to boarding school at so young an age—and Roy was only about five years old.

"I do recall Roy crying once, at Waverley Train Station," my uncle told me, "and I remember comforting him on the train. But I think in general we enjoyed the school in the Borders whilst we were there...it was a large house and farm, 'Greenhill', I think it was called, somewhere near Kelso."

Once back in Edinburgh, Roy and Robert often walked together to school down Hanover Street and Silvermills Lane, but Robert has little memory of Roy at the school itself, not surprisingly, for the age difference between them would have meant separate classrooms and peer groups.

After approximately two years at the Academy, Robert was sent to Cargilfield School (then evacuated to Perthshire) and Roy went to Angusfield in Edinburgh, either as a day boy or as a boarder, for he was home quite often at weekends.

"Roy was a cheerful, outgoing boy, with a charming smile, whereas I was rather shy, solemn and reserved. He was much more adventurous—whether climbing rocks at the sea-side—or doing what he had been told *not* to do!"

With the freedom of a holiday in the Trossachs (around 1943) Robert, Roy, and one other boy found themselves down at a jetty by one of the lochs. They had been warned, of course, that under no circumstances were they to go out in the boats by themselves. Robert, being the eldest, took this responsibility quite seriously, and with a wild adventurous brother like Roy, it was understandable why!

Roy immediately and with great enthusiasm climbed down into one of the boats with his friend. Robert reminded them of the promise they had given: to his consternation, this was met with desperate pleas, and I dare say, muttered accusations of "spoil sport!" Robert stared down at the eager upturned faces of the two adventurers below, and with quick-thinking foresight, came to a suitable compromise.

"You can paddle out in the boat, but only for the length of the painter (rope), and only if I stay here and hold the end of it."

Whooping with glee the two boys vigorously paddled the boat, strong muscles pulling hard on the oars. Soon the little craft had picked up a good speed, and as the slack rope sprang taut like a whip cracking, Robert dug his heels into the rough wooden planking of the jetty, and hauled backwards, only to find himself flying out of control *forwards*, and head-first over the side of the jetty! With a huge splash he hit the water and surfaced to see the astonished face of his brother.

As the still-moving boat pulled him along, it occured to Robert that he might be going to drown, but luckily he ended up in shallow water and on the shore.

What Robert remembers most about this incident is that their father was called up from Edinburgh to 'speak' to the boys about their misadventure, and the folly of disobeying parental advice!

When, sadly, in November 1944 their father died, not long afterwards the boys left their schools and were sent to Basil Paterson's College School (whose main work was extra tuition cramming pupils for specific exams), and here they were privately tutored. "...I have happy memories of walking along to B.P.'s with Roy chatting away beside me. It was relaxed and easy".

It was the time when both boys depended on each other the most. Their father was dead (not that they had seen a great deal of him before) and then their mother 'strange', in a hospital for quite a long time, so that they didn't see anything of her for almost a year. Relatives and friends stepped in, and the boys stayed for a few weeks or months with them. When their mother did come out of hospital, Roy and Robert were sent to Aberlour, and then to Gordonstoun.

"We didn't have much contact at Gordonstoun, different classes, of course, and different 'houses', and we had different friends. But we were together all the time during the holidays." Holidays were spent in Edinburgh, and Roy and Robert often went on very long cycle rides. The red sandstone library at Stockbridge also held them spellbound for hours, as they selected many books on favourite hobbies, but it was to the large and irresistible pond in Inverleith Gardens that they would make regular journeys. With its silver rippling surface glinting in the sunlight and flashing with darting shoals of minnows, it was great attraction for many children, and cause for family get-togethers and picnics. There was a model boat club and a lot of these tiny vessels were not mere

letter home from school — aged 11

Dear Mum

I had a lonely birthday. Thank-you for the cake it was very good so were the sweets. I am eleven now. There was a thunder-storm this morning but I think it will be quite a good day my brother's boat goes [illegible] well.

I am getting on with my cricket. I can at least hit the ball.

LOVE FROM ROY

toys but replicas, built in beautiful detail; Roy and Robert were very keen on sailing their own model boats and had endless fun racing each other.

For Roy it became much more than a passing interest: Robert told me that they studied every book that they could get hold of — books on tea-clippers, barquentines, schooners, Blackwell frigates, in fact just about anything written regarding boats and sailing. It was this spark of enthusiasm at such a keen impressionable age that was to stay with Roy all his life, and later to be so vividly expressed in the seascapes he painted and the shanties he sang, (and of course, as those of us closest to him knew, in the humorous 'drawn-from-life' stories he told).

"As you know," my uncle confided, "Our Mum could be rather odd. Sometimes, just a day or two before the end of the school term, when we were looking forward to free time at home, she would phone the school to say that she would not be able to have us home for the holidays. This happened when we were around thirteen, fourteen, and seventeen years of age."

The school did well to cope at such short notice, and immediately arranged for the boys to stay with an understanding married teacher for a few days whilst something a little more definite was fixed up. Usually this was a short holiday with one of the younger members of staff, or arrangements were made for them to stay with an aunt, uncle or another relation.

"I don't remember being surprised or disappointed by Mum's actions (but I must have had some repressed feelings), and I don't recall ever discussing it with Roy at the time."

Although this strange distancing from their mother was to leave Robert with a quiet reservedness whenever she was mentioned in later life, in Roy it left a sense of bitterness bottled up and bound with distrust, and was probably responsible for his reclusive private lifestyle in his adult years.

Perhaps children are different — they are opportunists and survivors, and thankfully can be unaware of the deeper effects of estrangement, whilst carrying on with the tremendous importance of having fun.

Roy and Robert were not only brothers, they were friends, and on one Christmas holiday they joined the headmaster of their school and his family, and then went on to a hotel at Newtonmore for New Year. For Roy and Robert, it was wonderful. Snow lay thick everywhere. The hotel lent them skis, and they trudged through the blue-white landscape, feet heavily crunching in the snow, with plumes of misty breath, the sharp cold making their faces glow, as they headed for the hills.

At the top, they strapped on the skis, and went straight downhill at crazy exhilarating speeds, yelling, with no style— and certainly not much elegance! ...Unfortunately they were spotted by some of the Adventurers (competent and skilled skiers) who quite rightly thought the two lads, with their highly erratic and 'kamikazi' style of skiing, were a real danger to themselves and to anyone else who happened to come in range of these wild flights. (The hotel suddenly 'discovered' that the owner of the skis wanted them back...unexpectedly of course!) Nothing deterred, they were soon speeding down more difficult, steep, and bumpy slopes...but on a borrowed toboggan this time.

Robert well remembers Roy's exhausting battles with asthma:

"There were many nights he would sit up for relief, and ususally for most of the night. But he didn't like people fussing over him or it, and already by the age of thirteen was buying his own remedies; odd-smelling inhalents as well as the standard Ephedrine."

Roy was considered to be allergic to butter and for quite a while didn't drink much milk either. One of the things their mother excelled at was organising a healthy diet, and supplementing this with a large supply of vitamin and mineral pills,

Gordonstoun Hockey 2nd XI, 1954
Roy, second from left, back row

so, for the knowledge available at the time, he had good care.

Despite such a handicap as asthma Roy played hard, Robert thought he might even have made the first team for rugby at Gordonstoun. He never complained about being short of breath, but most of the time he was happiest if just left to cope with asthma by himself.

Roy was also interested in drama when at school, and although he never played any significant roles in the school plays, probably the grounding he learned from this interest set him at ease when later in life the stage became a familiar friend indeed!

Once, when he was little, and ill in bed, Robert heard him talking to himself from behind the closed bedroom door. This was somewhat alarming, and he alerted his mother. They both sat on the stairs outside Roy's bedroom, and quietly listened.

Roy's voice crescendoed and softened, as he talked on and on, in one long monologue. It was very good: sounding like the recital of some play, but as they listened and made out the spoken words, they suddenly realised that he was reading aloud the four-line doggeral that in those days appeared below the pictures in some comics! But it was the way it was spoken with such liveliness and feeling that had been so puzzling.

I asked him what were his first memories of my father's interest in music? He paused for a brief moment before replying,

"Almost the first photographs of Roy as a little boy show him with a musical instrument...a miniature squeeze-box; but the first time I can recollect him playing music, was when he had been given a small mouth organ as a stocking filler at Christmas. Later, he used to go out into the hall of 62, Northumberland Street, (cold though it was) and play it there

'...almost the first photograph of Roy as a little boy show him with a musical instrument — a miniature squeeze-box...'

for the accoustic effect. I became very impressed with his occasional variations of simple tunes by the time he was about fourteen."

Their mother played the piano regularly, and Robert remembers listening to her, not formally but just as a background sound. Although he himself had taken up flute-playing at school, (he gave it up after a while as he felt that he was rather mechanical in his playing,) he has no recollections of them playing together as a family.

When an orchestral company would visit Edinburgh, their mother used to take them to concerts, and Roy in particular loved the wild flamboyant movements of some of the more energetic conductors, (and when aged about eight or nine years old, he was so impressed that he then used to 'conduct' orchestras that he heard at home on the wireless); and later, at night (Roy and Robert shared a room), they would take turns to try to guess which song or tune the other was tapping out as a rhythm on the headboards of their beds.

watercolours and drawings of Roy's, done on visiting cards, aged 13

Robert's earliest recollection of Roy's interest in painting went back to sometime in 1945. In searching for a birthday present to give his mother, Roy had chosen a watercolour painting by the artist Stephenson. It was a scene depicting a country cottage, and sometime later they both set out to copy it. Robert remembers being considerably surprised when his mother thought Roy's copy better than his own.

"I thought perhaps, at the time, it was a reflection of his thoughtfulness in remembering her birthday. But I am now sure that it was because his was so strongly painted, an effective presentation of the same scene. (I had thought it was too strongly coloured and distorted, but in truth, mine was the laboured mechanical copy!)"

They drew and painted a great deal as children, and Roy was still painting a lot by the time he was about thirteen years of age. Rumaging around one day, they came across a stock of their mother's visiting cards, and Roy immediately set to work on a series of small pencil/crayon drawings and little watercolours of ships on them; and there was real team work at Christmas when the greeting cards were made by Roy with hand-drawn sketches, and the message and lettering inside being Robert's handiwork. Robert adds,

miniature seascapes, aged 17

"I was very fond and proud of Roy's paintings, and for years I carried a small snapshot of his first-ever oil-painting around in my wallet. I am very glad to have that painting now, painted on an oblong scrap of unprimed plywood."

Although she was sometimes labelled eccentric, a little bit strange, or rather 'odd' in her mental attitudes or views, in her own way my grandmother did try to be a mother to her sons, it was just that more compelling interests and ideas sometimes held sway. She did care that they should have good careers, even if Roy tried to block her interest. I suppose she was best summed up as being a great mother...but only on occasion!

She was sufficiently keen to encourage Roy's obvious talent for painting, and it was to this end that she took both her sons to visit Dr Robert Lillie, a well-known Edinburgh collector of paintings (especially those by W G Gillies), to ask him what would be best for the fifteen year old Roy, by way of advice about painting.

He told Roy never to say that a painting wasn't for sale, but

Roy's first oil painting

if he didn't want to sell it, just to put a ridiculously high price on it, and that way he probably wouldn't sell it; and if he did, well, he'd get a real windfall! Further, the high price of sale would help establish that his paintings were really worth a lot.

Robert remembers that visit well, not so much for the advice on painting, but for the stories Dr Lillie related to them. They had all been admiring his collection of paintings, and had settled down for afternoon tea. Dr Lillie told the two boys a horrific story from his childhood, when having been stricken down with appendicitis he was put on the kitchen table and the operation to remove the appendix performed there and then!

Later, Robert and Roy expended a lot of agonised thought over Roy's portfolio for a place at Art College. At this point

Roy was rather disenchanted with his mother, and she was given little say in the matter, although Robert says that she would have had a good eye for the paintings, as well as imagination. Roy did get a place at Art College on the basis of his portfolio alone, regardless of what his 'A' level exam results might be be.

Roy went to Art school and Robert to College, and as adults, they saw less of each other, but though distance kept them apart, they never forgot about each other, and whenever contact could be made, it was. When they met, the old protective reserve went on like armour, but it was flimsy like a brilliant light being concealed under muslin cloth. Their great affection for each other, and their immense pride in each other's successes shone through vividly. Having had a basically very unstable childhood, they represented the solid foundation of family for each other. Having found the world to be an untrustworthy place when they were in their teens, they learned trust in each other.

more of Roy's miniature seascapes, aged 17

My father's first love of his life was the sea in all its flighty and untamed moods. He spent part of his young adult life working at sea and was lucky enough to witness the last great echoes of the tall ships in working use, unlike today when they are more for training, charter and display, and with increasing costs, becoming ever more rare a sight. Dad loved the wooden decks, the pitch and tar smell, the strong jute ropes and the crack and boom of the wind in the sails. Many of his experiences are remembered in his songs, (such as *The Reivers Galley,*) where the keen-ness of his senses recorded each exhilirating moment.

Apart from working at sea, he also spent time employed in the seine-net boatyards, and later he taught seamanship at the Moray Sea School. But he felt equally at ease in the countryside, and I think a love of stone and fossils and a respect for nature came to him more by way of an education, rather than work, whilst employed in a quarry, then later forestry. Dad used to laugh at all my funny stories of my own work on a neighbour's farm; but I never realised then that Dad, too, had helped out a farmer with stock and tractors when he was young, and I suppose for him it was his youth recollected through mine.

The love of the sea lured him also in art. He worked long and hard to capture the storm-tossed spray and fierce bite of a North Sea wind on canvas, and to encourage him further, people asked to buy his paintings. This brought in a small amount of income but, much more importantly, he realised that his art had future possibilities. So he knuckled down to hard work and painted furiously. He enrolled at Edinburgh College of Art in 1955 and was there until 1959.

3

My father was successful at art school, and exhibited paintings in Britain and the USA. It was at art school that music really came to the fore; (to quote from one of *The Corries Song Books*, 'Edinburgh College of Art...was the beginning of the story of The Corries') and he formed his own skiffle group there with Robert Marshall, after studying to play the guitar. (Mind you, he was hopeless at reading music, but his good ear and quick memory taught him far more.)

The Casa Arts & Crafts Group, formed by Roy in 1960 —
(from left to right: Roy and Violet, David Harding, Peter Stitt and Sheena Manson)

And it was at art school that he met fellow painting student Ronnie Browne, —but more often they met in the rugby matches at weekends, when Ronnie played for Boroughmuir and Roy for Edinburgh Wanderers (on the wing).

Also at art school he met another fellow student, Violet Thomson, and they married in 1958. They lived at 18 Fettes Row, where Dad became very keen on photography, building his own dark room, constructing an enlarger out of coffee tins!

I came along in June 1959, two weeks before my parents graduated from Art College. Dad then did art teachers train-

ing at Moray House after which he taught art at Liberton School, Edinburgh, until 1964. When we moved to 69 Northumberland Street, near my Grandmothers house, Dad formed a ceramic workshop in the basement, having been prompted to take up pottery at Moray House. He designed and built the potters wheel himself, and with David Harding (ceramic artist), Peter Stitt (painter), Sheena Manson (mosaic and glass) and himself, (painter and potter) he formed the Casa Arts and Crafts Group, which exhibited very successfully all over Scotland; (The Ceramic workshop was later moved to Henderson Row).

Holiday travels to Europe had taken him to Spain and suddenly his guitar-playing crescendoed into life in a magnificent and inspiring way, through the wonderful flamenco music. He studied the guitarists and their instruments —he was already very influenced by Segovia—and learned more of the

(opposite page):
Roy the photographer:
Art College graduation photographs taken by Roy at Northumberland Street
(far left): self-portrait, holding his diploma, (his suit still crumpled from packing during the move from Fettes Row) and
(right): Vi

(right):
a favourable review from Sydney Goodsir Smith

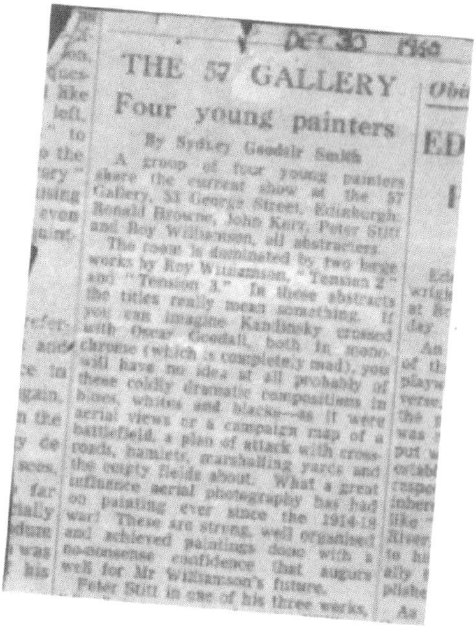

DEC 30 1960

THE 57 GALLERY

Four young painters

By Sydney Goodsir Smith

A group of four young painters share the current show at the 57 Gallery, 57 George Street, Edinburgh: Ronald Browne, John Kerr, Peter Stitt and Roy Williamson, all abstracters.

The room is dominated by two large works by Roy Williamson, "Tension 2" and "Tension 3." In these abstracts the titles really mean something. If you can imagine Kandinsky crossed with Oscar Goodall, both in monochrome (which is completely mad), you will have no idea at all probably of these coldly dramatic compositions in blues, whites and blacks—as if were aerial views or a campaign map of a battlefield, a plan of attack with cross-roads, hamlets, marshalling yards and the empty fields about. What a great influence aerial photography has had on painting ever since the 1914-18 war! These are strong, well organised and achieved paintings done with a no-nonsense confidence that augurs well for Mr Williamson's future.

Peter Stitt in one of his three works,

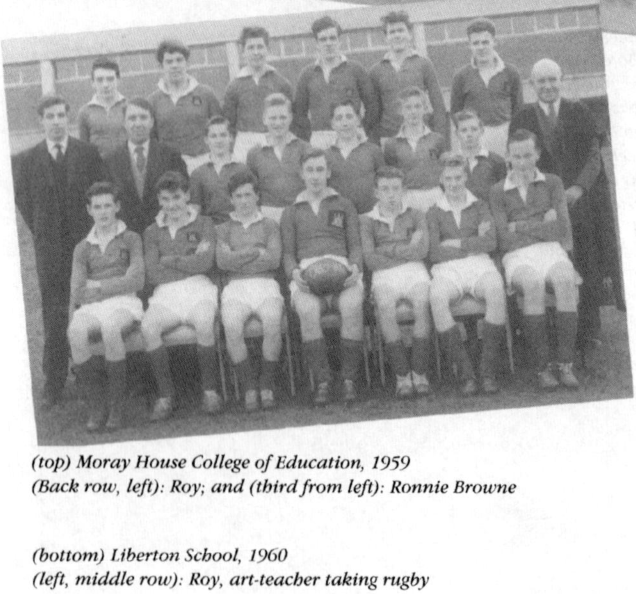

(top) Moray House College of Education, 1959
(Back row, left): Roy; and (third from left): Ronnie Browne

(bottom) Liberton School, 1960
(left, middle row): Roy, art-teacher taking rugby

art of making a guitar.

Always creative, his love of music inspired him to make all sorts of guitars throughout his life and he loved to enhance them with fine detail such as mother-of-pearl inlay.

I remember, as a child, tiptoeing into the studio when he wasn't there and seeing the old fashioned planes for shaping the wood, and the curled, clean white shavings with the new-wood smell and texture like stiffened paper. I remember, too, the fear of being caught in the 'forbidden zone' but the allure of exploration tempted me on, and there, in a box, the pieces of mother-of-pearl, like a treasure trove at last uncovered, its smooth satin surface alive with running rainbows and flashes of light.

From far off came the booming call:

"*Karen*?"

I was discovered! At least discovered to be missing from my room and toys. I knew my very silence had given me away. It was well-known that if I was silent I was up to something!

I jumped with guilt and scampered with great haste as fast as I could from the studio, before it was noticed that I had actually been in **there**! But yet I made an unspoken vow to visit the magic box of rainbow colours and crisp wood shavings whenever the opportunity presented itself.

Dad's growing expertise in this craft of guitar-making led him to experiment, and he began to make quite a few innovations of his own.

Bill Smith had also been at Edinburgh Art College, where he won several awards in architecture. However, he had a family background in music, as his father played the fiddle and the rest of the family were quick to accompany him. At impromptu ceilidhs Bill often appeared in Edinburgh, his birthplace, and although qualifying from Edinburgh Art College as one of Scotland's most promising young architects, he never abandoned his music.

The Corrie Folk Trio — Roy, Ronnie and Bill Smith

As a child my memories of Bill Smith are very few. I seem to remember him as an angry young man, but that was probably more likely because of my childish, constant interruptions to rehearsals, for Dad too, on occasion, could be an angry young man! I do remember Bill Smith's clarsach, it was a little Irish harp, and my mother told me not to touch it...

Well, what do you expect?

There it was, lying on top of a box in the corner of the room, and there was I ...alone!! I strummed it, softly at first, savouring the tinkling singing of the strings, up and down the scale of it. Of course I hadn't a clue how to play it, but the sound of it was wonderment to my imagination and hearing. My fingers caressed the strings lightly, then snatched sharply at one or two. Sometimes a discord of clashes, sometimes a pretty series of accompanying sounds. I was spellbound and, had I been left in the room for ten years, I might have learned to play it: but, as usual, I was located and banned from the harp.

I probably knew Bill more through his wife Etive, and their children Sean, Neil and Corrie, as I quite often played with them and we had great fun when left to run riot in Aberfeldy a few years later—but that's another story!

Around 1961, Bill formed The Corrie Group merely on an experimental basis, with Ron Cruikshank, and Roy, and then later, with Paddie Bell, they became known as 'The Corrie Folk Trio and Paddie Bell' and gradually established themselves. Dolina MacLennan, I have been told, recalls that their first public appearance was at the Waverley Bar, Edinburgh, where she was at the time the resident singer. On that occasion she asked them to play in her stead as she was to be away singing with Jeannie Robertson in Inverurie: and for this first public performance they received the princely sum of thirty shillings (the equivalent of £1.50)—to be split between them!

Ronnie Browne joined them just prior to the Edinburgh Festival in 1962.

The 'icing on the cake' was Paddie Bell. Even as a child I remember her pure sweet voice, together with the instrument backing from Dad, and the harmony of Ronnie and Bill. The effect was dazzling even for me. Paddie's voice was untrained, natural and the nearest thing to the heavenly choir I could envisage. I've never to this day heard one to match it. She held us all spellbound, you could hear a pin drop in the silence of the audience as they listened to her Irish tones and lyrical imagery.

Gradually their popularity on stage and in concert led them to their first-ever television appearance on the McEwans 1963 Edinburgh Festival Show, and that same year they were contracted to Waverley Records, with the release of their first EP. But it was in 1964, after they were signed up by the BBC for *The Hoot'nanny* television show, that The Corrie Folk Trio and Paddie Bell became professional, gave up their jobs and started touring up and down the country with concert work, and also appeared on television with the *White Heather Club*. Paddie Bell left the group not long afterwards to settle down to family life, and then Bill Smith left after an angry disagreement at the end of 1965.

I must admit it was lovely to hear that Bill Smith, Paddie Bell and Ronnie Browne had sung again together during the 1992 Edinburgh Festival, all quarrels forgotten, and a real joy to be back in each other's company. My mother went to see them and was most amazed.

"It was incredible, Karen," she told me on the phone.

"In what way, Mum?" (—her enthusiasm pricking my curiosity).

"Well, over the years The Corries changed a little—the style and type of music they sang, for example."

"Oh, surely not that much."

"Oh, Karen, when they first started Roy was the gifted instrumentalist but didn't do so much of the singing, it was really the other three that harmonised."

(Mentally, I tried to envisage and 'hear' that sound.)

Mum continued, "So when Ronnie, Bill and Paddie started singing the 'old' songs it was as if we were in a time warp. It was uncanny, unnerving and beautiful."

"What did the crowd think?" I wondered.

"I'm sure a lot of them were the old crowd returned, and it was as though thirty years had disappeared and we had gone back to our young days."

It must indeed have been a 'good gig' and I wondered if I would have enjoyed it. I probably would, but there could have been a painful, sharp note of discord for me to see the empty space where Dad should have been. But then again, who knows, perhaps he was there in a way.

4

As the wind-torn autumn of 1992 started to give way to the first still frost of winter, I decided to visit my mother and grandfather in Edinburgh, to research information on my father that would enrich the childhood memories I had. The next few days were worthy of being entered in an Olympic competition, as I rushed to meet this person or that, and by the end of it all, lack of sleep was beginning to wear me down.

Mum arranged for us to have lunch with Paddie Bell, so I felt it would be lovely to hear some tales of Dad that I hadn't heard before. Paddie lives in a beautiful Victorian house, not far from the centre of town, and yet beside a park fringed

The Corries Folk Trio and Paddie Bell

with trees. Her home is bright and cheery, and tastefully hung with paintings; her husband, Sandy, is an artist and an architect. Music pervades everything at Paddie's home, and although there was no sound of it at that moment, its influence surrounded us. Records, a music centre, in one corner a dark elegant piano, and at its feet a couple of other instruments asleep in their protective cases.

Paddie is a very small person. Mum used to describe her as 'elfin-like', and when you get to know her, it is a very apt description. Her gentle Irish lilt almost a whisper, yet full of laughter, and bright care. She has a very cheery personality that seems to flow into other people around her.

We settled down in the sitting room, after a light and nutritious meal. I wondered if Paddie would object to my taping our conversation, partly for extra information for the book, but also as a personal keepsake of stories of Dad. I need not

The Corries Folk Trio and Paddie Bell

have fretted. Paddie was at ease, and spoke in a relaxed manner.

As a child she had always enjoyed singing, but the connection with The Corries happened around 1962. Paddie at that time worked for The National Trust for Scotland, and one evening she and her husband were invited to an architectural party. The host knowing of Paddie's gift for music invited her to play the guitar and maybe sing something. Flattered at the invitation and probably slightly nervous at all the attention focused on her, Paddie duly obliged and delighted the party goers. Then the host introduced another young guitarist and asked if he too would entertain. The dark-haired young architect was announced as Bill Smith. He played the guitar like no other, his fingering fleet, skilled, and yet effortlessly. Paddie was quite impressed but then so were the rest of the crowd.

It's a strange thing, fate, because that chance meeting between Bill and Paddie led to the start of The Corries with Paddie Bell.

newspaper cutting showing the late Jeannie Robertson singing with the Corries Folk Trio and Paddie Bell

Later that year Bill contacted Paddie and asked if she would like to become lead female singer in his group... As I have already described, the first venue was The Waverley Bar in St Mary's Street, Edinburgh.

"At that time the group consisted of Bill, a wee chap called Andy, Ron Cruikshank, Roy Williamson and myself. Subsequently we had a lot of rehearsing to do with all the new material, but the group sounded really good. I remember the Clancy Brothers were really impressed when they visited Roy's flat, and happened to hear us. Finally, after all the preparations the evening arrived for our concert at The Waverley Bar. We wondered what kind of reception we would be given, and to our delight, there was a terrific response from the crowd there.

"Time passed by, and unfortunately Ron Cruikshank contracted glandular fever, and Andy too had left the group, but we asked Ronnie Browne (who had a fantastic voice, especially in high harmonies) to join us. This is when we become known as The Corrie Folk Trio and Paddie Bell.

"Not long after this we were offered a show during the Edinburgh Festival in a coffee house called The Tryst, in the Royal Mile in Edinburgh, and we gave three half-hour performances a night. It was really fantastic, and the group was going to earn £15 for the entire three weeks of the Festival! By now long queues were starting to form for our performances, and people patiently waited in line right down the High Street. We could hardly believe our good fortune. This was to be my favourite Festival ever, though of course we did quite a few more over the years after that".

Paddie could recall those exciting three weeks with vivid detail. She remembered how they walked around the city with their guitars, and as people began to recognise their faces, they would flock to The Tryst to see them perform each night.

Such success demanded fitting transport to ferry the musicians to even more venues...and so the 'Corrie Car' arrived! It was a two-tone green Jaguar, with a sweeping back to it, and it carried them safely to their next gig at the Gleneagles Hotel. At the time the £20 they earned for that show seemed an incredibly generous amount of money!

As they became more experienced as performers, their popularity began to scale new heights. They were called to an audition by W. Gordon Smith. Many other people were there to apply as well as The Corrie Folk Trio and Paddie Bell. Because of the number of people there, they decided to leave a publicity photograph with him. Quite a few months passed, and the group had heard nothing at all and felt they must surely have been forgotten. But meanwhile W.Gordon Smith had been busy organising the production of a new Folk show,

The Corrie Folk Trio and Paddie Bell at Cappo, Ireland

a series in fact, called '*Hoot'nanny*'. He asked his secretary if she could remember any of the people who had auditioned all that time ago? She thought for a moment then replied that she had a photograph of one of the groups in her desk, And it was this lucky break that introduced The Corrie Folk Trio and Paddie Bell to their first televised performances.

(Some of the telegrams still remain that they had been recieving before this, from both BBC television and Scottish television turning them down—before W. Gordon Smith 'picked them up' and promoted them on *The Hoot'nanny Show*!) *The Hoot'nanny Show* series was shown every Monday at 6.30 pm on the BBC national network, for a wonderful twenty-six weeks! The recordings were very good, and The Corries had guest artists appear on stage with them; people such as The Dubliners, The Spinners, The Ian Campbell Folk Group, Ray and Archie Fisher, Nadia Cattouse, and many others besides.

Such was the success of *The Hoot'nanny Show*, that the following year Gordon Smith created another televised performance, a series called *Sing Along*. The Seekers, The Settlers, and Julie Felix, were invited as guests this time, as well as a few of the performers who had played on *Hoot'nanny*, including special guests like Tom Paxton, Ewan McColl, and Peggy Seeger.

Paddie chuckled, "When we were recording a programme, rehearsals always stopped for lunch, from twelve-thirty until two o'clock. The Dubliners, of course headed for the nearest pub, and at two o'clock there would be not a sign of them back at the recording studios! I remember Gordon ordering me to, "GO and find those countrymen of yours in whatever pub they are in, and tell them to get back here as quickly as possible!" When I found them, they turned to me and said, "Tell Gordon we will be back around 2.30—when the pub closes!"

"Another rather amusing moment, during these programmes, involved a double bass player called Tony. At one of

the recordings, I was singing a very sad song called *Lord Gregory*. It called for subdued lighting and no external distractions from the crew or other performers. Suddenly Tony, who was due on next, realised that he was on the wrong side of the studio. Right in the middle of my sad atmospheric lament, all I could see was Tony, between me and the camera, on his hands and knees, pushing his huge double bass across the floor. It is very difficult to be unobtrusive with a double bass at the best of times, and it was equally difficult for me to keep a straight face and finish the song!

"On the strength of the series, we all gave up our jobs to become professional and of course, because of it, we were well enough known to embark on tours all over Britain. There were two tours each year, one in Spring and one in Autumn. The touring was absolutely marvellous, especially in Scotland, where the scenery is so beautiful.

"We always practised in the car, working out harmonies, etc. When people say that to be paid for doing what you love is fantastic, it really is true!

"Life was so carefree and enjoyable. There was one agent who arranged our tours and he sent us all over the country at breakneck speed. For instance, one night we would be in the Liverpool Philharmonic Hall and the very next night in

Aultbea in the West of Scotland! When we arrived in Aultbea, Bill said, "I can't see any hall anywhere here at all," It transpired that we were to play in a Nissen hut!

"When we were touring it was off season time for hotels, and some of them were very damp and cold. Bill used to say that if you leaned your elbow on the bed, the hole filled up with water, and he wished that the owner would stop growing mushrooms in the mattress! He always had a great sense of humour.

"We once went to the Orkney Islands to do a concert, and this meant the 'Corrie Car' had to be lifted onto the ship in a big net. At that point we were all getting our pens out to sign autographs for the admiring crowd, when to our consternation and embarrassment, two of the mudguards fell off our 'deluxe' transport as it swung onto the ship!

"I was very afraid that I would become seasick as the journey was supposed to be very rough. Timorously I asked the Captain for some advice. The somewhat startling reply was that I should have a large brandy and port... Well, I did this...and the sea was as calm as a mill pond, but I was incredibly ill—because of the brandy and port!

"When we were doing a tour in Ireland, we went to O'Donoghues pub, in Merrion Square, Dublin. It was teeming with musicians—The Dubliners, The Clancy Brothers, and a lot of other famous names. I remember I was sitting next to Bill Smith, and there was one seat left beside me. A tall man wearing a black suit came in, and sat down. By way of conversation, I asked him, 'Do you sing or play any instruments?' He answered, 'I play the guitar, and the long-necked five-string banjo.'

" 'Isn't that strange,' I exclaimed, 'I've just bought one of those myself, with Pete Seeger's initials on the vellum!'

"All this time I had been aware of Bill poking me in the ribs, so I turned and asked him, what was wrong now?

" 'Do you know who you are talking to?' Bill asked.

" 'Of course,' I quickly answered, 'He's an American gentleman, who likes folk music.'

"Bill hissed quietly to me, 'That *is* bloody Pete Seeger!!'

"During one of The Corrie tours in Dublin, we did a gig at a dance. We were really quite chuffed with our performance, and Roy said to one of the wee girls that had been dancing there, 'Did you enjoy that?'

"She replied in her strong local dialect, 'Youz were mank!' ...It kind of killed the conversation!"

Paddie has a real gift for seeing the funny and light side of life, and her tales of the fun the fledgeling Corrie Folk Trio and Paddie Bell were tangled in, as they climbed the early and not always easy road to success, brought to life for me the youth of Dad and his fellow performers. Sometimes it was as though I was discovering things about Dad and The Corries that had somehow passed me by, as a small and unaware child. Paddie carried on with a couple of funny stories about Bill.

"Once, when we were away on tour, Bill announced that he thought he might be going down with a cold." (This is every performing singer's nightmare, as he relies so much on a clear voice and good lung power. Something as simple as a cold can really jeopardise a tour timetable). I told Bill I had just the thing to sort him out, and gave him a Redoxon vitamin C tablet, which was a big as an Alkaseltzer and very effervescent. When I looked round a wee while later, he was foaming at the mouth, and I thought he was having some sort of fit!

" 'You might have warned me to put it in water!' he gurgled.

"During those early days of tour time, W. Gordon Smith was producing our records at Waverley Studios. I remember during one recording session we had to sing a sad song called *The Bonnie Earl O'Moray*, and when we came to the line that reads, '*They hae slain the Earl O'Moray, and laid him on the green...*,' Bill softly added, '*Two yards from the 18th hole...*' Well, we tried and tried to record that song but every time we came to that line we giggled uncontrollably. Finally we had to leave it and come back on another day and record it then.

"Once we went to a folk festival in the south of Ireland, in a place called Cappo. Roy's wife Violet, and Bill's wife Etive came with us. We were upstairs, in our bedroom overlooking the street, when suddenly an old battered car rumbled and clattered to a halt outside, and all the Clancy Brothers poured out. Everyone ran out to meet them. There was such grand spontaneous music that night in all the pubs, and flowing out into the streets as well. That's Ireland for you!"

I asked Paddie if she could remember the first record she made with The Corries?

"The first ever was not an official one, if you like!" she exclaimed, a grin creeping across her face, "At bus stations and railway stations, there were often small booths, much the same as a telephone booth, or one of those passport photo booths, and you could record your voice on a tiny record, they were usually used to send loved ones a message. But The Corries all squeezed into the booth (and *that* was no mean feat, I can tell you!), and recorded a song on a very scratchy record...the sound quality was not the best either, as you can imagine."

Paddie started to look through her extensive collection of all the professional records she had made, and I marvelled at the wonderful songs from away back, but must admit to having a chuckle at some of the covers showing Dad with an old-fashioned haircut, or a howling gale whistling round the group.

When Paddie asked why I did not have any of these records, I replied that I knew Dad saved two of each record he made, so that Sheena and I would eventually have a collection each, but somehow amid all the turmoil later in life, the collection must have been given away, for we never saw the records again. But Dad was diligent in seeing that we had the

Dreich conditions! The Corries Folk Trio and Paddie Bell recording on a cold wet day in Edinburgh

later ones from the time when Ronnie and he became The Corries. Okay, we occasionally had to ask again, or he would tap his head with his hand, grin and say,

"Oh, God, I forgot again! Ah, well, you know what they say about the cobbler's bairns..!"

"No?"

"The cobbler's bairns never wear shoes, meaning the obvious is always the most often overlooked, just keep reminding me!"

We did, and Dad brought us the tapes and records, and even some for me to use as a raffle prize in one of the charities for which I was raising money.

Yet somehow I long for those haunting songs of the far distant past, that surrounded my tiny years, and enveloped me in a cloak of care and love. They are not just tunes, they are a passport back in time, and my adult mind only retains snatches of the words and harmonies.

Paddie thought that it was sad that we didn't have the early collections, and kindhearted as always, she offered to tape some of hers to give to us. I was really touched by that, especially when she is so busy, and I was very grateful.

I wondered if Paddie could remember any of the funny things that must have happened when they were on tour? Things like props breaking down or mikes not working?

"Not really..." She thought carefully, then brightly added, "Once we were performing in another country, and the lighting man there was deaf, and he kept getting the sequence of lighting completely wrong. He was supposed to use the blue lighting for sad songs, and red for the loud funny ones...

"Well, the poor man couldn't get it right! We would be up on stage with a packed house of eager fans looking up at us from below. As usual we started with a loud cheery song to get the audience stirred up, and as we sang we expected the bright rosy spotlights to quickly flash down on us. To our horror, the lights dimmed so far down, they almost went out, we could hardly see each other, but we bravely carried on, loudly strumming guitars, and roaring out the chorus, as we were softly bathed in sad blue spotlights... Then the mood changed, and gently picking sweet, sad, notes from the instruments, we began a soft lyrical lament,—when all of a sudden the lights burst into a high intensity set of bright and cheery red beams...completely at odds with the song!

"Yes," Paddie smiled, "we had our share of humorous moments."

In the early days of The Corries, when they had to speedily transport themselves up and down the country, Ronnie was the only one who could drive, and he was a good, safe driver too. However, Roy asked to be allowed to have a shot, and after a few words of instruction, Ronnie moved over to let him try the car. Roy was *not* very good, and I think apart from the odd yell of alarm, the rest of The Corries sat silent and extremely tense, knuckles gleaming white as they hung on. The stretch of road was a very scenic one that climbed steeply, with great drops into bottomless chasms below, and to further compound matters, Roy was learning to drive on hair-pin bends with the possible risk of another unseen vehicle out of sight just up ahead!

All too soon my visit to Paddie Bell was over. I thanked her and Sandy for their good-hearted hospitality, as we made our way down the long hall, with its wonderful Victorian floor tiles, and great open fireplace, where once travellers would gather the warmth like great folds of a cloak about themselves before riding off into the night air. Paddie gave me a hug, and a few promises about keeping in touch, and then we left, stepping into the bright but cold winter's sun. I glanced back and they waved, still smiling, these people from my childhood, whom Dad had known so well.

Mum was on a high too, but for her it was more in the way of bringing to life her young days, when she travelled on tour with the rest of The Corries Folk Trio and Paddie Bell.

5

Then, on New Years Day, 1966, (after a successful Trio appearance on BBC TV's *Hogmanay Show*), The Corries, Roy and Ronnie, played their first performance as a duo at the Royal Jubilee Arms, Cortachy. Bill Smith had left after a disagreement the night before.

Roy and Ronnie, without Paddie — and now without Bill — had to make a decision. To carry on, now as a duo...? Risky, and unknown territory. Or to do what they had been trained to do initially, that is to return to teaching Art at schools in Edinburgh. (Roy having taught at Liberton, until *The Hoot'nanny* television series had allowed them to 'go professional').

Both of them had already endured five years of frustration in teaching. Not so much with the kids they taught as with the stiff, tight regime of staff rules. It had reached the point where their inspired ideals as newly-fledged, qualified teachers were depressed and restricted, and over the years little incidents began to grate on the nerves and become blown out of proportion. Something had to give, and the teaching had, and The Corrie Folk Trio and Paddie Bell had arisen from those ashes.

Yet things had now come full circle. Could Roy and Ronnie face teaching again?

No. Instead, they decided to give 'The Corries' a go.

(Yet still in a way they were teachers too, because all age-groups flocked to their concerts and the young learned, not through paint and canvas, but through lilting music and creative words. The pictures imprinted on each mind traversed time and legend in a hues of colour and mood.)

And as The Corries, they became wildly successful and their

photo: Graham Falconer

The Corries: Roy and Ronnie

popularity went from strength to strength. Dad did a lot of song-writing for the duo and was the main instrumentalist, and Ronnie ran the business side, with the help of Lee Elliot, his brother-in-law, who was stage manager (amongst a variety of other roles). The Corries did not have a huge 'ground crew', they tended to do most things themselves or with a few friends. I think this is why it all worked out pretty well, because they knew at each time who was responsible for what. And whilst working hard on tour they dealt intelligently with crises and tensions along the way, so there were not the wild arguments that usually tend to arise when people have to be constantly in each other's company in a working situation for such a long time. One secret was the 'No contact'

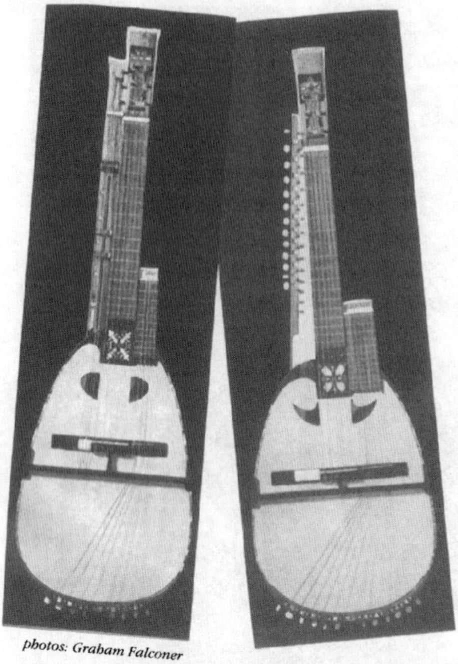

photos: Graham Falconer

The Combolins

rule that they did their best to stick to during their summer breaks; it gave both a chance to unwind and relax with their families, then, renewed and keen, they met up for the next tour.

And those tours took them to far-off places, to little villages and crofts, or large halls and theatres in the cities. They entertained all over the U.K., including the Albert Hall and Festival Hall in London, (also the Savoy Hotel where they topped the Bill for three weeks) and then abroad to Canada and the USA (1971, '75, '76, '77 and '78), as well as Germany and beyond as far as Australia, and still their fame grew.

Being surrounded by different musical instruments all my life tended to insulate me from the individualism of each one, and the entirely different skills needed to create such marvellous sounds from them. I suppose it's a little like the person brought up in the town who has the awareness of green spaces of the country, whereas the country person is dazzled by the lights of the city.

Whenever he could, Dad would find out about different instruments and learn how to master them. One of the last ones was the fiddle. He was totally self-taught, bar a few hints and pointers from friends now and then. His instinct and his 'ear' made each session better, and more craftily intricate, although initially there were sometimes tortured strains howling from the attic...

The guitar was the main love of his life, and he would often sit down to watch the news, relaxed and automatically playing the most finger-tripping flamencos of his own creation. We called it 'Dad's fiddly music', because it was so incredibly complicated, but great to hear. (The nine o'clock news later seemed so stark without its musical backing!)

Spanish guitars, twelve-string guitars, on a rare occasion for fun an electric guitar, he loved them all but was thirsty for one better. So he created the twenty-eight string guitar. Haunted by the peculiar and thought-provoking sound of the Indian sitar, Roy felt that the drone effect from sympathetic strings in response to played strings, had a Scottish ring to it. The twenty-eight string guitar looked nothing like a sitar — for example it had a short neck and large rectangular body compared to the elegance of the long-necked sitar. But after a lot of effort, many disappointments and mistakes, much retuning and changing of strings the twenty-eight string guitar produced at last some of the sounds he wanted — or very nearly!

Ever the perfectionist, he strove again to invent a wonderful, wider source of musical sounds, and built the two Combolins. They were an amalgamation of three different instruments in one, in order to allow for a change of instruments half-way through a song without disruption. The Combolin for Ronnie to play had extra bass strings on one neck, then a normal guitar playing neck, and finally a mandolin one to complete the effect. His own Combolin had drone strings, a guitar playing area, and a bandurria section. The Combolins each had their three necks side by side, and were fairly long to accommodate the length of strings. The large span of hand needed to for their various frets and chords made their playing an art that not one everyone could have accomplished.

The bodies of the Combolins were large and bulbous to give the sound box full scope and the strings a good anchor at the base. But they were not just functional, they were beautiful too. The artist in Roy Williamson embellished these wonderful creations with ivory and mother-of-pearl, and dark sections of wood to contrast with the golden gleam of at the base of the instruments. Antique mahogany was used for the necks of the Combolins, where as the decks were made of Tyrolean spruce and the sides of sycamore. The bridges of ebony contrasted vividly with the rosewood, mother of pearl, silver wire, ivory and copper inlay. Two months to design them were followed by an incredibly hard two months of actually building them. But soon they became recognised for the individuality of The Corries craft in music, and the Combolins, like *Flower of Scotland* will long be linked with Roy Williamson and The Corries.

Mum introduced her daughters to their father's marvellous work, she thought the Combolins were wonderful and she was proud and pleased for Dad. They became an inevitable excuse for a brawl between Sheena and I as to which of us wanted the Combolin with the 'sad eyes' or the one with the 'angry eyes'. (These were the holes in the deck for sound.) I think Dad just rolled *his* eyes heavenwards!

Other instruments Roy and Ronnie played included many different types of whistles, flute, mandolins; Ronnie also played the harmonica, and the banjo; and both of them played the bodhran (borann), an Irish hand drum played with a sheep's tibia on the drum's surface of calf skin, producing a wonderful throbbing rhythm, and in the audience a real stirring of the blood and thoughts of sailing galleys or a march to battle. The Northumbrian pipes produced the Scottish bagpipe sound but had the ability to be restful, soothing and quiet, which could enhance the sad ballad, or crescendo in the fighting songs. I don't remember much about the zither guitar, but Dad's concertina was a well-loved instrument: like the guitar, he loved to play it while watching the news (but you tended not to hear the news at those times!)

To me, the music spoke of sea shanties and storm-tossed fishing boats, or the crew's cabins and mournful journeys far from home. But most of the time it was jaunty and brightened your spirits, and, if so inclined, your steps as well! Sometimes Dad would play a wee ceilidh with my mother's father on the accordion, and perhaps Sheena and I with 'spoons' or 'pots and pan' drums! Good fun certainly.

Dad wrote many songs including of course *Hills of Ardmorn* and *The Dawning of the Day*. He also wrote the theme (and played the concertina) for W. Gordon Smith's film documentary about Gavin Maxwell in the early sixties.

But think of The Corries and you think of one special song: *The Flower of Scotland*.

Dad told me that he wrote *Flower of Scotland* with just

two verses initially, and didn't think much of it at the time, so he stowed it away in a drawer, probably just before 1965; and it was not until The Corries were short of material one day that they then tried *Flower of Scotland*. Dad worked on some more music for it. My mother says she remembers him first creating the tune on the Northumbrian Pipes (and as they can be fairly loud I dare say she wasn't likely to forget it in a hurry!) but he played *Flower of Scotland* on the bizouki for the first public performance of the song.

The audiences loved it more and more as the years passed, it became adopted as the Scottish National Anthem, and it was sung by many thousands on the terraces of football and rugby grounds world-wide. It was a true folk song, chosen by the people, *they* made it such a success. Even so I still swell with pride that Dad wrote it.

I think *The Flower of Scotland* was first recorded in 1969, I can remember Dad sending me a postcard from on tour, he was so chuffed that *Flower of Scotland* had risen quite high in the charts against all the pop songs, it had got to no. 2 or 3!

Of course, the real glory came during the Grand Slam in March 1990 when the Scottish rugby side won against England and more than 50,000 people sang an emotional and proud *Flower of Scotland* at Murrayfield. The atmosphere that day was incredible, and standing amongst all those voices singing my father's song would make anyone proud to be Scottish.... and for me, well, just being his daughter makes me proud. For after all Roy Williamson's patriotism and craft, his inspiration and goodheartedness and his courage in strife, for me he was the best of Scotland...the Flower of Scotland's heritage.

An extract from Roy's notebook, on Flower of Scotland:

This is God's Acre, our home. The most beautiful country in the world, bar none.

One doesn't accept money for honour. If my fellow countrymen have chosen my scribbled thoughts and music for themselves then it becomes theirs.

I wrote the words and music, made the song inspired by this country of ours — Ronnie persuaded me it was good enough — but it's the people who made the anthem — not me.

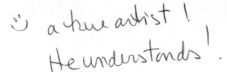

6

Not so very long ago, when I was down in Edinburgh, I found out a little more about the early years when Dad and Mum first got together. My mother's main impression of Roy, the first time that she met him, was his athletic build and fine sense of fashion.

"He always seemed to lead fashion in those student days, and was fond of wearing a blazer and flannels, I always thought that he may have been the first to set the trend in American baseball boots for casual wear — it was not long before the trend caught on everywhere!"

So there was Roy Williamson, handsome, athletic, leading the student fashion scene, and being gifted in art and music

Roy, 1955, first term at Edinburgh College of Art

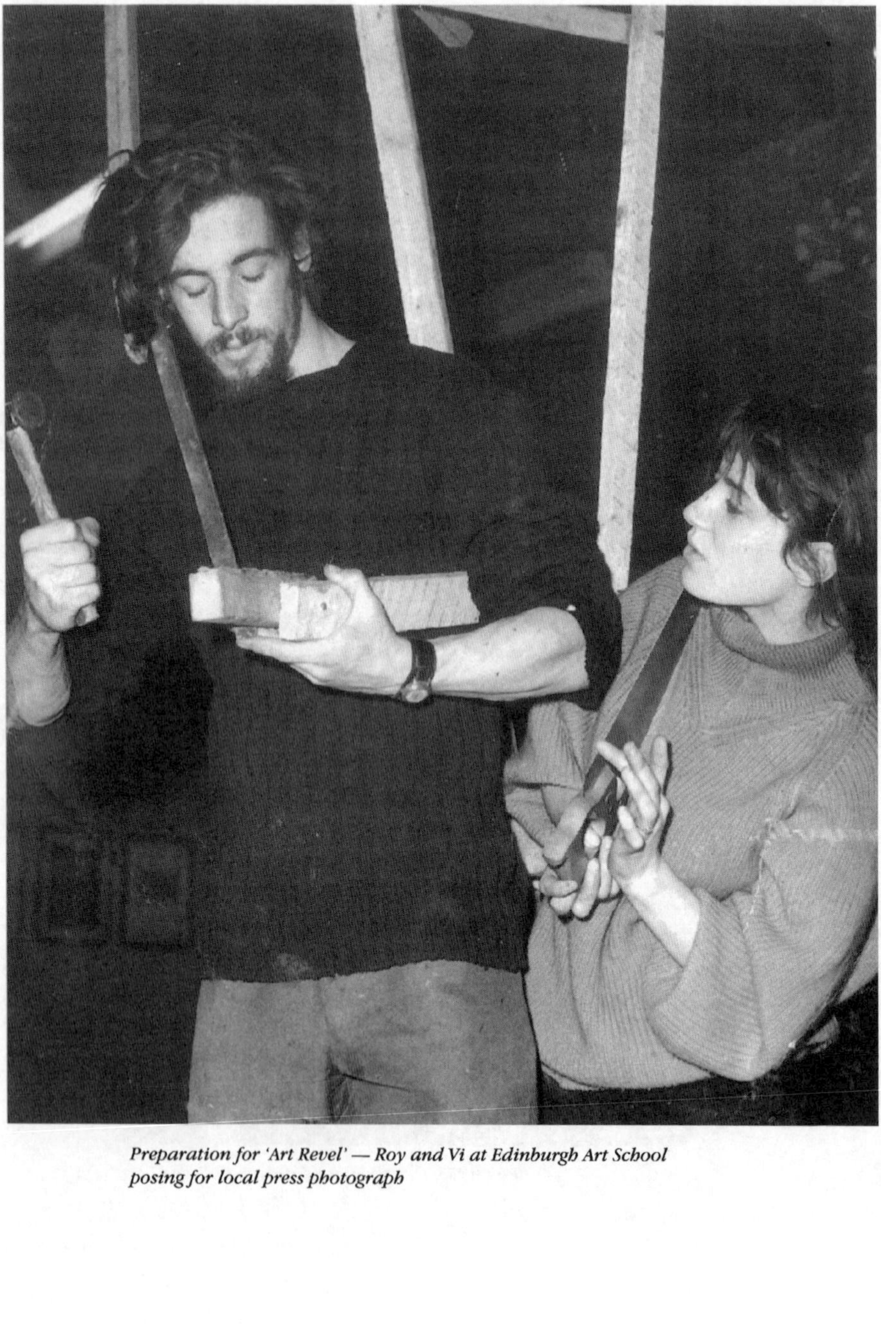

Preparation for 'Art Revel' — Roy and Vi at Edinburgh Art School posing for local press photograph

as a bonus. My mother, beautiful herself, also liked to wear flattering clothes, but it was really their love of art and music which gave them more in common. They were a well-suited pair, and together they were invited to most of the parties and social get-togethers.

She was at ease with Roy's mother, (which was more than could be said for Roy, apparently they were always at loggerheads, his mother continually critical of her son). Her first impression of her was of a tall and very elegant woman, with the most beautiful delicate long hands, (perhaps why she was so talented at the piano). I gather my mother was a little overawed at first by the magnificent Georgian house in Northumberland Street.

"What did you like best about it, Mum?"

"There was the most amazing wood panelling in the house," she explained, then added,"It was rather unusual for a house to have such panelling at that time, and it's still there today."

"Is it? How do you know?"

"I've seen it!"

"What, recently? Have you been in?"

"No, no!" she replied flippantly, "I've had a look in the windows when walking past!"

I smiled, how like Mum, disregarding protocol!

"Roy used to play the recorder at Art College, and he was very good at it. I can remember him sitting up at a window, playing a beautiful, soothing rendition of 'Jesu, joy of man's desiring'. It was not until a while later that he managed to save enough to buy his first guitar. He mastered the first three chords, but that was about it, until Bill Smith taught him a tremendous amount. I always admired Bill's natural talent in producing effortless and magical music from the guitar, and he proved to be a good tutor to the raw keen-ness of Roy."

I think this was when Dad became interested in trad jazz and skiffle groups and at a time, so my mother informed me, when just about every college up and down the country had a couple of skiffle groups to its name.

"Roy loved Lonnie Donegan records, and that kind of music was a massive influence on him, and contributed to his success with the skiffle group he had formed at Art Collrge. But I still maintain that the foundation of his musical genius stems from those early guitar lessons when Bill Smith introduced him to a whole alphabet of chords, rather than his basic three. From then on his musical career began to take shape, and he invested in a Gibson twelve string (steel strung) guitar, which gave an even better sound to his skiffle group."

Another major influence to the 'Williamson early technique' was Big Bill Broonsie, and also Josh White, the folk/blues singer; Roy used to sing some of Josh White's repertoire, such as *Trouble in Mind*, and of course more traditional ones like *Banks of Ohio, Streets of Loredo*, and *Kisses Sweeter than Wine*. Alan Lomax's *Take this Hammer* was another favourite at that time; Alan Lomax, folk song collector from America, came to Scotland and met Hamish Henderson, and together they went around collecting songs from this country. Hamish Henderson (of the School of Scottish Studies) was a fund of information, and Mum still has a soft spot for him. "Hamish was very helpful to Roy. He is such a goodhearted person," she said, in recollection of the years when help freely given to young, struggling students meant a great deal. Hamish played an infuential role in Roy's musical development and encouraged him and introduced him to other folk musician's work.

"His main influences," she continued, "were Skiffle, Traditional Jazz, Dance Bands, American Blues, Burl Ives and some African styles of music, and not least, Flamenco, and Segovia. But don't forget that Roy was just one very ordinary person with an interest in music, he was just a young lad of his time...there were hundreds of others, just like Roy, doing the same kind of things in Art Colleges in Glasgow or Dundee, or right up and down the country, and in America too."

"So how did you feel later about Dad's rising success in The Corries?" I asked her.

"Well," she hesitated, thinking back, "'The Corries' came much later, we were just art students in those days, as far as we could see art was going to be our careers, music was the way we enjoyed our free time, that and going to parties or dancing."

"Dancing? Was Dad a good dancer?"

"Oh yes, he was one of the best at jiving,"

"Oh, not that awful thing where you threw each other in the air, or over each other's shoulders?!"

Mum laughed, "It wasn't that bad, you know, in fact Roy was very good at it. Strong, athletic: he was brilliant."

I was not convinced, as I began to remember the photographs I had seen of jiving. To my prudish mind it all looked very dangerous and silly!

Dad was involved with Edinburgh Harriers, an athletic organisation, which accounted for his degree of fitness. He had even thrown the javelin for Scotland, in his quest for success at whatever pursuit interested him during certain periods of his life. He was a perfectionist, and it was this same drive that helped to make his music so good in later years; but also this same drive that caused a short but uncomfortable year of non-communication between myself and my father later in my teenage years.

7

Born in Nairn in 1935, my mother Violet Thomson was the eldest of three girls. Her father, Willie Thomson, had led a hard working life on the farms around Moray and the Black Isle. He and his wife worked from dawn to dusk, six to seven days a week, and she worked as hard as he did over the years as a help on the farms, milking goats and cattle the old fashioned way, by hand, or looking after chickens and helping with the work in the farmhouse. There was always laundry, cooking and housework to be done.

When my mother and her sisters were very young, the Thomsons moved to a bleak location just outside the scatter-

Out jiving in Inverness in 1957 — Vi and Roy as art students

ing of houses called Dalwhinnie, where Balsporran Cottages nestled beneath great, towering, windswept mountains, sparsely covered with heather, coarse grass and steep scree. And yet there was a wild cruel beauty to the environment. Where the winters were cold and totally isolating, community spirit was more than friendship, it was a necessity, a life-line. Grandad by now had left underpaid work on the farms and as the more profitable railway ran right beside Balsporran, he became a worker for British Rail, eventually ending up as Ticket Inspector. He loved the trains and the people who worked with them. 'Beel Thomson' as he was known had that forward and incredibly funny down-to-earth sort of humour. He has to this day the Highland pride and hospitality, and the ability to laugh at his own mistakes. You feel at ease and welcome in his company, and my father always made a point of going to see Grandad when eventually he and my Granny had retired to Edinburgh.

Recently, my grandfather wrote a letter to me describing the first time he met Roy Williamson, my Dad. The promised letter duly arrived. My grandfather spent much of his youth amongst the soft-spoken Highland folk, with a simple, but hard working life on the farm. I think his Highland accent and thrawn and witty mirth sparkles in his descriptions.

> Dear Karen,
>
> Enter Roy Williamson, 1957! This young man entered my life round about this period when he was an art student in Edinburgh, along with my daughter Violet. I always remember him as handsome young lad. Anyway, you walk through life, and you don't know what's in front of you, so there he stood, and I found him to be quite a gentleman, one who was on the threshold of starting to make his own way in life.
>
> He had just finished college term; now I'm not sure what exactly happened at the 'breaking up' party, but I was told they all had a bit of a celebration and a wee bit dram!! Roy was not a whisky drinker at that time, and his pals were saying, 'Come on, Roy, drink up!' But he

wouldn't. Anyway as far as I can gather, they began to taunt him, saying, 'You can't take it, Roy!' So Roy put out a glass, and he downed it in near enough a 'one-er'. That was a very bad drink for him, as he was troubled by asthma, and he was really ill.

Violet, his girlfriend at the time, said 'Come and see my Dad, and he might help you.' So he arrived here at our home, and he had to go straight to bed, where he lay for nearly a week!

Finally he was up and about, and I lent him one of my racing bikes to see if a run out into the country would give him a bit of colour. I took the spare bike and went with him. I knew everybody in all the crofts along the way; Bill was our first stop. He had about twelve cats and just as many pigs; and that day he was sitting at the

Vi's father, Bill Thompson, photographed in his eighties

Roy (centre) and Vi (right) and her sisters on Nairn beach in the fifties

pig sty, with a pig on his knee, stroking it like a pet kitten! We left Bill's and cycled on to his nephews, who were all great musicians and had played on the radio in Aberdeen their Scottish Dance music.

We cycled on again after that, and met an old pal of mine, who was a fair hand at the violin. He had a tame owl, and it was amusing to see it standing on one leg with a dead mouse in the other. Roy really enjoyed himself, and was not far behind my bike on the road back home again.

The next thing I remember about Roy, was when he started up his pottery. The only transport was a Cycle Master which was only about 25 c.c., so we carbonised it, and next day he set off on his journey to Fort William, to meet someone there who had an interest in pottery. He actually made it without a breakdown, and that was a journey of over sixty miles, and the front wheel of the bike was egg-shaped due to having hit a rut on the way! I think it was more like riding a horse, rather than a bike, I tell you he was glad to get to his bed that night!

His interest in pottery grew and he started making ashtrays and jugs and all sorts of other articles which were very good indeed. He was very clever in many ways, and when he needed a lathe for turning the pots we went to a scrap merchant of and obtained a big wheel off the clutch of a tractor. Roy assembled a steel stand of some sort, and he pedalled to make his table rotate, something like a gramophone; and with clay and burnt ashes he made fine glazes.

After the Cycle Master, we qualified for motor bikes of 125 c.c.; I remember I had the first one, which was a BSA Bantam, and Roy wanted a shot on it, so I told him to get a licence, which he did; and he took off, the only trouble being when the bike stopped, the lights also stopped...they went out! The police caught him without lights and poor Roy was fined. After that he got a bike of his own, and we used to have nice runs all round the country. We went down to the Forth Road Bridge, which was barely complete at the time, and we never dreamed he would one day be playing at the Grand Opening of it, The Corries in their infancy.

Castle Tolmie was a huge house that I was offered by a friend. He said he'd sell it to me for the bargain sum of £300, but he could easily get a thousand for it. So I said, 'If you can get a thousand for it, why are you giving it to me for only £300?' He replied that he knew I could make a good job of it. Then Roy came on the scene, and he was quite interested, so he said to leave the legal side to him. By this time the purchase price had been reduced to £100! Roy contacted architects and surveyors, only to find that the house had been condemned six months previously, and had we bought it we would have been responsible for demolishing the building, costing hundreds of pounds. He was a good friend to have. Yes, Roy and I could tell you a few wild stories from over the years.

Did he remember the first time Dad was ever on stage?

"Och yes," he chuckled, "it was at the Staff Association in Inverness and your father was supposed to go on and play a wee bit of guitar."

"What do you mean, supposed to...did he play it?"

"He took fright, he was very young and awfully shy at the time, and he stood in the wings and refused to go on."

"Poor Dad, how embarrassing..."

"— Ah, but just you wait," Grandad scolded me for interrupting, "Your mother went to lead him on, she picked up the mandolin, though God knows what she thought she was doing with that as she hadn't an ear for music! Anyway your father went on that stage, and I joined them, playing the mouth organ, the crowd were totally unaware of what a near thing it had been: it turned out to be a fine old ceilidh!"

Inverness 1958 — the wedding of Roy and Vi.

He grinned away to himself, lost in his happy memories. "Another time your father was staying with us in Hilton, Inverness, and we had a fire-surround at the coal fireplace that had a seat attached at each side. Well, your father used to sit there playing the guitar and singing, and the kids from outside used to come to hear him play, but they didn't want romantic Scottish songs, they used to yell out to him,

"Can you no play 'Davey Crockett, King of the Wild Frontier' for us?"

I asked my grandfather to tell me about the wedding between Mum and Dad.

"Weel, you know," he said in his soft Highland accent, "your father had been going out with Violet for some time, and then one day he came in, formal-like, and asked to speak to my wife. So they both went into the kitchen, and a wee while later, my wife came through to see me. 'Willie' she said, popping her head round the door, all excited, 'Roy's wanting a word with you. he's wanting to ask you if he can marry Violet!'

"I checked with my wife how she felt about this, then asked her to call Roy through, and we had a wee chat about how he was going to support her, and my own worries that I wouldn't be able to afford the wedding, being as we were fairly poor at the time. Your father, too, didn't have much money, so the wedding day was put off until funds could be raised. Then, when the money became available, the wedding was arranged to be held in Inverness on March 25th, 1958."

My grandfather went on to explain that as the day drew near he became terribly nervous. Things started to go wrong...the minister let them down, and there was the biggest panic finding another to stand in. By this time Grandad felt his nerves getting the better of him, so he sprinted off to a chemist (normally you couldn't get him near such places!) 'Och, man, my daughter's getting wed in the church up the road and I'm shaking like a leaf, have you anything that will calm me down? It's an emergency!' The chemist gave him two green pills. Who knows what they were, but they certainly sorted Grandad's nerves, which was just as well, as it seemed as if the whole of the country town of Inverness had turned out to watch the procession of bride, groom, family and friends parade up the street, and they gaped at the the crowd of Edinburgh art students with their fifties-style 'drain-pipe' trousers, funny suede shoes, and long blazer-type jackets, but I think it was the strange hairstyles that amazed the quiet country folk most — had the Teddy Boys hit Inverness!?

The wedding was held in a little church just below the academy. Grandad had arranged for the Williams Trio (a well-known accordian band who were very good, having performed a lot on radio) to play for the dancing, "They began to play, and of course your mother and Roy had to dance the first waltz by themselves with everyone looking on, and they were not very good at it! Roy couldn't waltz to save his life."

"It's a pity it wasn't jiving," I joked, "he'd have been okay then!"

"Then the whole place came to life with everyone dancing. It was a really good band, great music, and your uncle Robert was into his sporran for the drinks for everyone. He was very generous, he's a good man you know. Then the skiffle band got up, and as your father played great skiffle, everyone had a whale of a time, Willie McKay joining in and getting everyone going as well!"

"Who's Willie McKay?"

"Willie McKay was your father's best friend!" Grandad retorted as if I should have known that.

Many hours later, after yet another sing-song, I think Grandad's little green pills must have been working well because Grandad was still entertaining everyone, not a nerve in sight!

I asked where Mum and Dad went for their honeymoon, romantic notions of Spain, France or even Italy running through my imagination.

"Och, the Drumossie Hotel in Inverness!"

On vacation in London — Roy and Vi, Easter 1958

8

My mother had worked as a window display and price-card designer in Inverness, when her family moved there from Balsporran; and then went on to Art College in Edinburgh. She was a slim beautiful girl, long, dark hair, grey-blue eyes, with a talent in art and the ability to socialise with all crowds of people, and a good dancer, together with humour and an interest in music. People change with time, but both she and my Dad held onto their youthful good looks all their years.

She has always a peaceful attitude. Sometimes she becomes frustrated at the complications in life, and resents the rich having more while the poor suffer; I suppose she wants everyone to live in a caring family unit, where all things are fair and equal. She has a simple way of thinking, but don't ever confuse that with untintelligence, she is clever in a way that catches you off guard...suddenly...when you least expect it. But she is also admired for her humour: Dad's humour was incredibly funny and often evolved out of a short narrative on some experience or other. But Mum's is the one-liner type, a summing up of a certain person or misfortune in a dry and teasing way. There was no cruelty involved. It was just a funny slant that none of us had ever had the cleverness to think of ourselves.

Of course Dad's fame took its toll and as Dad was away from home more and more, his absences made communication strained between them, especially as financial pressures came to bear. And yet even after their divorce when I was about twelve or thirteen years of age, he was in every way a father to us, and encouraged Mum in her ideas or career moves, and was there to help her with his support if she failed. I don't think they ever stopped being fond of each other, it was just that they couldn't live with the pressures on their marriage. Something had to give. Dad retreated to his peaceful isolation, and Mum threw herself into socialising, making friends, and delving further into Art. Art was her medium of communication.

Watercolours were her best painting medium, and Dad used to like them a lot, and when she wanted to exhibit Dad helped her, he was keen that she should make a success of it. Another venture was her interest in antiques and she bought and sold some as a small business, again Dad backed her in this. He was immensely proud of her success in the Open University course on Art, and enthusiastic that she'd battled her way to a qualification with courage and skill.

Today my mother is still doing her bit for others, despite trying to make her own career in Art, and looking after my Grandad (on his own since Granny died). She also keeps a maternal eye on my sister, and with the usual enthusiasm and total ineffectiveness tries to discipline her grandson, David, my sister's boy! As usual she's too gentle and David, at six, is ready to explore and fight the world! Perhaps a shade of Roy's childhood spirit governs him...

She has always been immensely proud of Roy, of his musical gifts as well as his art work. Although she would fiercely defend him when criticised by others, yet she liked to analyse certain songs, or paintings, that he did, and it worries her that people don't know about the talent he had for pottery, nor of the beautiful pots he designed.

Just over a year after their wedding, after I came along on June 7th 1959, preparations went ahead to organise the christening, and I was dressed up in a beautiful white gown that had belonged to my father's family and which seemed twice as long as I was. In those early days my father had glasses; and he taught me, as a baby, to reach up and pull off his glasses, it was a joke to show me off to friends, I suppose, but it backfired the day I was christened when, in the middle of such a well-attended ceremony... I happened to

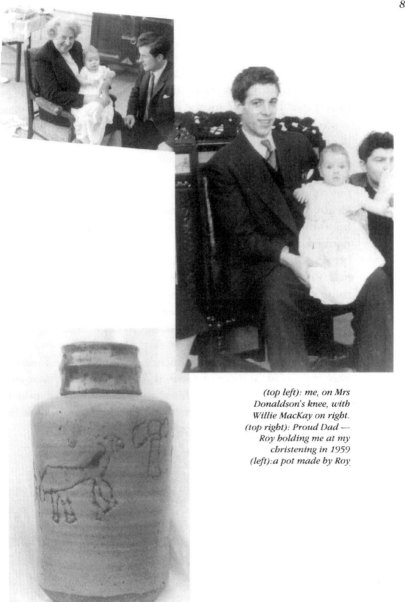

(top left): me, on Mrs Donaldson's knee, with Willie MacKay on right.
(top right): Proud Dad — Roy holding me at my christening in 1959
(left):a pot made by Roy

notice...yes...the minister wore glasses too! After the ceremony, everyone came back to the house, and a lengthy photo-session began, with everyone posing for the camera with me on their knee. I have this startled 'about to be sick' expression in all the photos, whereas the other folk's expressions vary from contrived earnest and important stature, to Dad's one of terror that if he moved he might snap me!

Mrs Donaldson's expression was the most relaxed, she had been Roy's landlady of his student digs. She took in two students at that time, and really gave them a happy family environment: Mrs Donaldson not only rented the boys rooms, but she was always cooking this and that for them, and never forgot anyone's birthday, and even let Dad paint with oils in his room. Oil paints have the strongest smell to them that permeates every inch of a house, it's a smell you grow to love because of the nostalgia associated with it, but for little old ladies used to home baking aromas, it must have been something of an intrusion. Mrs Donaldson was loved by all our family and the bond was never broken. I remember as a teenager going with Mum to visit her in her wonderfully old-fashioned, but spotlessly clean flat. Many people over the years were to have a great influence on Roy, people from all over the world, and famous with it; but to my mind, dear old Mrs Donaldson was one of his major influences, she gave a very young Roy some secure stable backing from which he was able to gain a lot of strength.

9

In the early 1960s when we lived in Northumberland Street, Edinburgh, asthma began to take its toll on me, but it took more of a toll on my parents who coped as best as they could with what was an alarming illness in a child, particularly in those days. To me they seemed unnaturally bothered, it was something I lived with since I was three years old and I knew no different way, had no concept of life without asthma or the

Roy, Northumberland Street c.1961

terrible consequences it could have for some.

Dad, asthmatic also, blamed himself for my asthma, he felt heartrendingly guilty that I had inherited it from him. It was something of which I could never relieve him (even as an adult I failed to convince him that my illness was not his fault, he couldn't help what was in our inherited genes, no more than I).

But then Dad was like that. Sometimes he bore the weight of the whole world on his shoulders in a most unplausible way.

Asthma had it's amusing moments too. I was made to smoke special herbal cigarettes and inhale the vapour of a burning powder that smelled very like incense. When I was particularly fractious Dad would tell me wild adventure stories of long ago battles. He'd tell me that the glowing pin-pricks of light in the burning poweder were the campfires of two huge, opposing armies, and if I looked deep into them I could imagine the people moving about. He was always full of super stories. There was nothing better than when he told me bedtime stories, and I'd struggle to stay awake for hours just to hear his soft voice enact a scene, or narrate enthralling imaginative descriptions. When he was on tour he arranged several stories from tales of Greek heroes on a huge old heavy tape recorder beside my bed, so that I'd still fall asleep to the sound of his voice.

When I couldn't breathe and sat forward in bed, hunched over and straining, ribs hurting as I gasped for breath, I would have to stay in bed, and became very irritable, bad-tempered and terribly bored. Both my parents being artists soon saw to it that I was provided with sketch books and crayons, and imagination further fuelled by Dad's stories, I learned to try to create marvellous images on the paper, (and, for a short unattended time, the wallpaper around me!). Once, when very ill, I slept behind a curtained section of the living room, probably so that they could administer an inhaler if I sounded at all 'wheezy'. For me it was paradise, because I could pull aside a tiny section of curtain and see all the forbidden television programmes my parents watched, when they thought I was asleep! Then Dad would catch me and tell me in no uncertain terms, "Shut your eyes and go to sleep NOW!" The inhaler was a weird thing, like a large air bladder, from which protruded a curved tube. When you squeezed the bladder the medicine was forced into the tube and turned into a vapour, which you were then required to breathe in. It was an old form of medication and I wondered if it was that, or a lack of oxygen, which caused me one day to see three foot high cartoon butterflies winging gracefully around my bedroom: Walt Disney would have been proud of me. However when I pointed them out to my mother, she couldn't see them. What — fancy missing three foot high butterflies, a purple one just missed her head by inches, this was very infuriating! It was not long after this event that my inhaler intake was reduced, and I never saw the huge butterflies again!

We used to go to church, or rather I used to be taken to Sunday School. I would swing on Mum and Dad's hands as we stepped off the kerb to cross the cobbles in the bright sunlight. The little stooped old lady was playing her hurdy-gurdy organ down the street, musical strains speeding and slowing with the crank of her arm and fading into the distance. Never failing to fascinate me, I would twist my head round as we passed and stare in awe at the woman's ruddy complexion and cheerful grin. Soon the huge red doors of the church would swallow us up, like the jaws of a whale. I have no memories of Dad in the church, just a few of Mum, before I was old enough to be entrusted to make the journey alone. Very soon my threepenny bit for the collection found its way to a strategically placed sweetie shop on route!

I used to enjoy the walks with Dad and Mum. Our milk was delivered by carthorse in those days and the huge horses used to fascinate me. Mum warned me one day by saying, "Don't go near that horse, Karen."

Here I am, plus new baby sister, Sheena

"Why not?" (I was always asking why).

"Because it's a white one!"

"Why should I not go near a white one, Mum?"

"Because white ones are always evil tempered and they bite."

I thought about that for years, and instead of frightening me away from horses, it made me reflect on the unfortunate circumstance of discovering that you had been born a white foal instead of any other colour!

There was one room in our house into which I was strictly

not allowed: Dad's studio. It was where he did his painting and songwriting. Often I would toddle up to the door and be tempted, but would always beat a cowardly retreat. When Dad would disappear to gigs and small concerts, and was Mum busy with certain chores, I would be left with the 'Au Pair' girl, who was usually Swedish and not good at English, and this led to great opportunities for 'misunderstanding' the poor girl! The Corries had really begun to take off now, and I was at last managing to sneak into the forbidden studio quite often, there to find Dad's favourite treat...a tin of Nestle's condensed milk (he had developed a liking for it during his Outward Bound mountaineering days).

For a while it puzzled him how the level in the tin kept going down...until he caught me one day, painting my red pedal car with a bottle of ink in one hand, and drinking the Nestle's milk with the other. That's the first time I can remember getting spanked, although being no angel I must have been so before.

I must have been five years old when Sheena, my sister, made her grand entrance on the scene on June 4th 1964. She was born at home, a process I found wonderfully riveting... well, all I could see, that is, peering through the keyhole in the bedroom door. Having been the only child and, I dare say, somewhat spoilt, it was a bit of a shock to discover that I had been ousted from my throne by something that resembled a prune! However the prune soon grew into another 'Golden girl' and I was quite proud *then* to show off to everyone that I had a baby sister. Wow, was that short-lived; until we grew up Sheena amd I were destined only to get on with each other when we joined forces against 'them', the 'unfair' parents, as we imagined them to be! Otherwise it was a constant battle for attention from our father, and as his popularity grew, he was more and more away from home, and he would bring us back presents. This created jealousy between my sister and I, as to who had the best present and therefore must be the one most favoured daughter!

Roy and Vi at Stirling Road

Mum did her best to be a good mother to her wayward daughters. It was easy when I was a baby because I did everything babies are supposed to do. But as I grew up and became fanatical about horses, it began to be a bit wearing on both my parents. I suppose I sought to communicate with Mum and Dad through my successes with the horses; and what I didn't realise was that I was boring them stiff. And if I thought they didn't seem quite as impressed as I felt they should have been, then I beavered away even harder at my chosen subject of horses and riding, hoping to make them proud. It must have dawned on them after a while that this child was definitely on the eccentric side! Whereas my younger sister, Sheena, grew up with all the normal interests of fashion, romances and teenage blues. Yes, we were a strange family, but nicely strange, and we never lacked for friends. I think people perhaps were drawn to our rebel 'break away from tradition' ideas.

I can remember when Dad came home with the 'new' car, it was the biggest car I had ever seen! What make it was, I couldn't say...just that it was big and black and backfired an awful lot. It could only go at about 20 mph and was happiest if you turned left and not right. But it was Dad's car, and he even washed it. And when we sat in it to go somewhere we were forbidden to speak in case he lost his concentration...we must have looked weird, driving at 20 mph in left-handed circles in total silence!

Both my parents were restrained in demonstrating their love for me, and this inevitably, marked me the same way. That's not to say we didn't love each other, it was just that we couldn't show it easily.

But in fact our lack of physical bonding enhanced our mental bonding. Just as a blind person develops a super enhanced hearing to compensate, my father and I developed a very sensitive sixth sense and telepathic ability. As I grew older this became much stronger...and it wasn't always a help! I knew before Dad came into the house exactly what frame of mind he was in; sometimes we would sit in silence but with the wild chatter of our thoughts running in 'duet' in our minds. Often I was able to voice his thoughts out loud, to which he'd smile; although neither of us valued such a gift. I suppose because we had always been able to communicate in this way,. we probably thought that everyone did. It wasn't much fun if he was furious about something. He'd talk quietly, but tersely, yet his mind and mood would thunder and storm in wild rages. It was awesome and overwhelming, enough sometimes to reduce me to tears, even if I wasn't the cause of it, and totally perplexing to outsiders who had not heard the communication between us.

Possibly he had developed this gift because his mother had kept his emotions suppressed, and as they could not be expressed so they surged and pounded in his thoughts. He stored a lot of worries, memories, exhilarations, moods, ideas and wonder, and I suppose instinctively, as a child, I learned to pick up on these.

During my most awful teenage stage I was most acutely aware of these, and then Dad and I had a hard time getting on with each other, and this was made worse by sensing the other's true rage, not the slight anger expressed in the spoken word! Good times were great and more than made up for the bad, but then too, for example even playing chess with Dad was not easy — as he knew my moves before I made them: and being new to the game I was still trying to remember certain moves that I had planned, so could not concentrate on what he was planning. But I loved those games of chess...what would I do to play one with him again!

Dad used to buy Sheena and me lovely presents; the kind any adult would be proud to own, but when I was the huge age of five or six, somehow collector's model cars or ice skates with a single row of wheels (instead of blades), were kind of lost on me! One year I was given a huge 'Make your own model boat' kit. I got as far as opening the box, Dad was enlisted to help and I didn't see the kit again!

He loved boats, the sea, and anything connected with them. He'd sometimes take Sheena and me down to Granton harbour at night. It was always cold with a damp, sharp breeze blowing in from the dark sea. The waves were oily black in the night, as they 'thwacked' and sucked at the wooden supports of the quayside. I remember standing on those wooden beams, being able to see the bottomless water beneath my feet, and being frozen with animal fear in case my next step would plunge the whole of me down through a two-inch gap that seemed more like a two-foot gap in my imagination! Dad would hold my hand, his grasp reassuring me that I could not fall, and we'd listen to the 'clink, clink' of halyards against masts as small boats bobbed in the water, or the lonely, haunting, deep wail of a boat far out, and the sudden roar and surge of white water as the Pilot boat came to life and set out, all lit up, to guide it in. Walking past the whaler we could hear the crew cheerily joking with each other as they sat down to a meal in the rusty, but warmly lit, cabin room. The stars would be out in the night sky and we'd get sore necks as Dad pointed them all out to us; and we searched for shooting stars.

10

17 Stirling Road was a huge Victorian house in Trinity, Edinburgh. It had endless stairs and the alarming habit of shaking every time a bus roared passed on the road outside. I remember Dad reassuring me, a twinkle in his eye, saying our house was built on an old rock which also ran under the road, this was why we felt so clearly anything thundering over it. Yet I remained convinced the house was haunted. One hour after everone went to bed the sound of slow footsteps would heavily creak up the stairs. Perhaps it was only the wood contracting, but to a child's imagination all kinds of monsters lurked behind the door! Dad was to eventually divide the huge house into three flats. The one upstairs he kept for himself and rented the other two out.

Dust clouds and dirt prevailed during the renovations and the beautiful, but spooky, staircase was done away with. I felt sad to see it go (but relieved that I'd no longer be troubled with the ghostly footsteps). Then a hidden room was found: well, actually it was more of a cupboard; Dad discovered it whilst sorting out the dismantling of the staircase. This little, walk-in room was empty, except for one thing... a model, life-like catamaran boat, such as people in tropical islands sail. Why was it there? How had it got there? Who owned it before? It was not a toy, and why had it been deliberately walled up? It seemed strange that Dad, who was so keen on boats, should be the one to find it. It remained a mystery, and he kept the boat and often marvelled at it.

The upper floor of Stirling Road was very much home to us. Not only were we minutes from the sea, but Dad, using all his talented craftmanship, converted the living room into a

Mum, Dad and me at Stirling Road

ship's interior. He used beautiful, mature, golden pine and at the windows he installed two narrow sofas, or settles, without arms or backs. The low-hung eaves, on each side of the two bunk-like sofas, and the walls were also lined in golden wood — you could almost believe you were in an old sailing ship. Dad quite often sat on one of the settles to gaze out of the window whilst playing the guitar.

At the opposite side of the room was the dining-room table, three huge pieces of mellow, golden wood fixed together to form the table-top, suspended from the roof by two beams: very much in the image of a galley table. On each side of the table were two more long settles in the same wood, with contrasting, padded-leather seat cushions. He was ingenious at making hinges, doors and shutters: each settle had a door on the end for storing things, and there was a super, experimental connecting hatch to the kitchen.

When, many years later, Stirling Road was sold and the new occupants moved in, I think he felt a wee pang of grief as they took out all that lovingly-created woodwork, and destroyed his 'ship'. But, always positive, he shrugged off any upset and focussed on the future, and indeed much later, the walled garden of his home in Forres exhibited even better examples of his woodwork in the doors and shutters there.

My schooldays arrived in a flurry of activity; smart, new — but far too big — uniform, ribbons flying loose in my pigtails, the special smell of my own brand-new leather schoobag, and new friends and playground games. Wardie School was not far from Stirling Road and Muriel McCance used to 'chum' me home. As time wore on I was beginning to have a serious problem with arithmetic; and this academic failure caused me hours of endless grief! Dad became more and more exasperated about it. Huge sheets of paper were pinned above the dining-room table, on the walls. On each, like the Ten Commandments, were all the multiplication tables. I had to stand and read them out loud before I was allowed to eat. Then one awful day...he took down the huge sheets, and told me to recite my tables — or I wouldn't get any tea!

"You have learned them, Karen, haven't you?"

"Ooh yes, Daddy!"

"Well then, start with the three times table."

I hesitated, felt panic start to rise and then...my mind went totally blank.

"Well, I'm waiting," (he had his stern 'not amused' look, denying me any chance of changing the subject).

"It's just..." I stammered.

"Just what!!?" he thundered.

"It's just that I've learned them so well... that I've forgotten them, Daddy!"

For days, following this frank admission of my genius, I was drilled in the times-tables (until Dad at least knew them perfectly!). In his frustration to pound the meaning of numbers into my brain, a box of 'Rods' was purchased and set before me. These were different sizes and colours to represent different values. These worked for a short time until my mind would drift onto how pretty the colours were, and could you build a tower out of them all? Poor Dad in desperation enrolled me in the Basil Paterson College, where I was dragged off after school, when all my friends were out playing! I was the only child there. Their methods worked a little, as the teacher was very nice and bribed me with peppermints. But at long last my parents were coming to terms with what a dunce their elder daughter was. I never fully mastered arithmetic.

11

With all my new school friends, I didn't lack for company and I was hardly aware that Dad was away more and more; but when he was home there were parties.

Sheena and I were always sent to bed early, but I became wise to this ploy! I would wait until the guests started arriving, then (timed to perfection)...make my entrance when they were all sitting down drinking.

"Mummy, Mummy, I'm not sleepy, I can't sleep!"

Mum would hiss under her breath for me to get back to bed, "This instant!". On cue, I produced the 'trembling lip' act and water-filled appealing eyes for all the guests. It never failed!

"Oh, do let her stay, she can sit on my knee!"

"Oh yes, Vi, let her stay!"

Thus was poor Mum coerced into letting me stay. It was wonderful. There were always candles flickering on the food-laden tables, the wax dripping in rivers down the wine bottles. And somehow a drink of Coca-cola and a bowl of crisps always found their way into my hands. Oh, I had this 'cherub charm' down to a fine art!

Everyone came. The familiar faces of The Spinners, the Dubliners, the Clancy Brothers, Barbara Dickson, Mike Harding (and many others, some of whom are whispers in the distance of time now). Marianne Faithful was another singer who visited us, around 1966, (when she was one of the guests on the *Corriefolk* show); although her first love was definitely folk music, she was successfully trying the Pop scene, where she became a very great champion in bringing the 'Pop versus Folk' separatism into a much easier integration. Mum remembers Marianne as probably being about

"I'm not sleepy!"
Sheena (left) and I in our dressing gowns, join the grown-ups party in the kitchen; the fiddler on the right is John MacKinnon

nineteen when she came to see us, in the days when she was with Mick Jagger. She and Dad singing played guitars together at our house in Stirling Road, sitting in the window seat in the top flat, singing favourites like *Mellow Yellow*.

And there was Jayasri Banerjee. I asked my mother,

"Who was the lady who came to our parties and played the sitar?" — the recollection of its eastern tones are very vivid in my mind.

"Jayasri and her husband came for the Edinburgh Festival. They were originally from India, but they stayed in London where she taught the sitar; she had been on BBC television and played recitals in Britain, and Anil Bhagwat and Suren Kamath were part of her group."

"I think Dad was quite impressed by the sitar, wasn't he? Did he try to play it?"

"Oh, yes — but everybody did then. George Harrison of the Beatles made it popular, but a lot of people who were interested in Indian music had gone out to India before him,

"...braw, braw, lads..." — *Roy and Ronnie*

yet because George was so famous some people thought that he had discovered the sitar. For example, Archie Fisher went to India, and he brought back the sitar and amazed everyone with it."

I mentioned to Mum that I had always had the impression that Robin Hall and Jimmie MacGregor were friendly competition for The Corries.

"Well," she reflected, "The Corries were very influenced by their style."

"Were they?" I was startled by this. "It wasn't the other way round?"

"No, no!" Mum exclaimed quickly, forcefully. "Robin Hall and Jimmie MacGregor were well established long before The Corries, they had great shows on television, they were very successful on that *Tonight* series they did — that was shown nationwide. What made The Corries so famous was the Folk revival movement that was sweeping the country at the same time as the Scottish sense of nationalism and independence was rising like a river in spate and nothing was going to turn it back. Apart from their natural talent as musicians, they were popular because a lot of their material was centred on Folk, and on Scottish nationalism."

I personally felt there was a lot of respect between both folk groups, and that whilst applauding each other's efforts, there was a friendly but wary eye on each other's camps!

It was touching to receive a card sent on by Ronnie to me after Dad's death. It was one of hundreds of cards which came here and it was from Jimmie MacGregor, who after all those years, had not forgotten a fellow performer and had penned a few lines of sympathy in memory of that link.

The Manhattan Brothers were from an African musical called King Kong. There were three of them who came to stay at our house, probably during the Edinburgh Festival, again. One of them, Chebacca, told me he was an African prince, which widened my eyes in childish astonishment and I shot off to verify this with Dad, who said, "Yes," but that in Africa there were many tribes, and each head of the tribe had a royal family. So I dashed back to Chebacca to find out what it was like being an African prince, and did he have to wear a heavy crown, like our Queen? Those brothers were the darkest coloured people I had ever seen, I was fascinated by them, not frightened, and certainly not racist. I admired them, they had a regal bearing and dignity and were full of stories of faraway places.

Those were the days when fame was just beginning to

sparkle and everyone was unaffectedly friendly. It was warm and genuine. Memories filter back, of gentle Barney from The Dubliners, who actually frightened me with his dark, thick beard and huge towering bulk, until he gave me a book on animals, and my fear vanished when I found the page about the sloth that climbed trees upside down! Barney explained the creature to me in his soft Irish voice and my eyes widened, my imagination lost in a dark, dank jungle of hooting, screaming and whistling animals.

The Clancys had wonderful guitar cases...and I discovered that there was a vague 'horse shape' if you sat in the dip in the middle. That's why, when my parents were chatting 'boring adult talk' to the Clancys, I was riding an imaginary black Arab stallion across a desert. Of the Clancys I do not remember a great deal, except wondering how on earth they wore such thick, white sweaters without itching like mad! — probably because I couldn't wear my own Arran sweater without some shirt between it and my skin.

The Spinners were great fun, playing Cowboys and Indians with me in the living room. I would shriek with excitement and run around like a possessed banshee! On one occasion I turned and pointed a finger at Tony, "Bang, bang!" Tony died brilliantly, but it was all too much for me! I really was convinced that I had shot him, and began to wail with uncertainty, embarrassment and fear. How often had I been told not to point fingers at people!! But it was okay, Tony came to life again with a grin. Sometimes the parties would move from house to house, and I'd be shrouded in a blanket, hoisted up onto the shoulders of the tallest of The Spinners and we'd all gaily march out into the glow of the streetlamps in the Edinburgh streets.

Robin Williamson and his girlfriend Christine, nicknamed 'Licorice', were good friends of my parents, they lived in a tiny flat in Edinburgh but they stayed with us at Northumberland Street on two occasions. They were both very young at the time, in their late teens. Clive Palmer and

not a stage performance! — fancy dress party 1962
(right to left): Roy, Vi, Ronnie and Pat Browne

Robin were the founder members of The Incredible String Band, but as the band became more popular it extended and Licorice joined it as well. (Robin also played for a bit with The New Lost City Ramblers but that was later on.)

I remember Robin and Licorice more as 'the giant adults' at the time that Robin was just starting to make a 'go' of things in the Folk music world, but of course that side of things didn't interest me at all then! What was absolutely mind-boggling and fascinating was the real, live fox they kept as a pet. Sheena and I used to love playing with the fox whilst all the adults talked about the 'boring' things adults generally seemed to us to talk about. Occasionally the fox would chase us, nipping our toes, and irritated adults would tell us to stop making so much noise.

Robin Williamson had a wonderful imagination, and once, despite being poor at the time, he gave me a birthday present I remember to this day. He'd made an old cardboard shoe box into a world of dreams by cutting a tiny square window at one end and covering it with sellotape and yellow cellophane, so that when you looked through it every thing became a sun-coloured place. Next he filled the box with different mosses and twigs and little pale-hued pebbles. For the final touch he placed a wee scrap of silver foil with minute ripples formed on it into one corner. The lid was put back on the box and pinpricks of light filtered down like starlight. I spent many a magical moment looking at my 'Tolkien' world and imagining great adventures there!

Robin had a considerable influence on my father's musical style and they'd have many practice sessions together. They both smoked a lot in those days, and would get quite high and be in a fine humour, marvellous pieces of creative music flowing from each of them, new and captivating melodies never heard before. Robin's view of what could be achieved opened up new paths of exploration in composition. (It was he of course who wrote *October Song* which Roy and Ronnie recorded in 1968.)

Martin Carthy was supposed to appear on a Corries show at the London Palladium, but due to a sad bereavement in his family just before the show was to go ahead, Martin had to cancel. Roy felt so sad about Martin's loss that he invited him and his wife Dorothy to come and stay whilst Martin was still recording *Sing-alongs* at the nearby BBC studios. And naturally, Roy, Robin and Martin spent a few hours practising music together, learning new techniques from each other.

Although my father and Robin were quite close in those days, as Roy's career began to take off in a big way and he became far busier, and had to meet more professional people all the time, the circle he'd moved in before became increasingly more distant, a thing of the past. I think the last time that Robin visited us was when we lived at Stirling Road. I find that sad, and feel my father should have done more to keep in touch with the people from his musical foundation years, but of course as a child I was never fully aware of the ever increasing pressures on his time until much later, when he was more and more away from home. But before that period, there must have been very carefree and wonderful days, when music was not a slave of money or practised perfection, but a thrill and a laugh, and a wonderment when something beautiful was created for no other reason than the joy of it.

Robin Williamson, too, became famous, not only with the Incredible String Band, but also on his own, with many successful tours in Britain and the United States. He was quite a driving force behind Friends of the Earth. A lot of Robin's inspiration came from the environment around him, just as Roy's came from the sagas of long ago.

12

My father was not great with children; yes, he could entertain them, but their immature conversation used to drive him up the wall. I remember one day, a very rare day, Dad had to take me to school on the bus. A thunderous mood had tensed silently within him, but I was hero-worshipping him regardless. That particular day he got into an argument with the conductor on the bus and started swearing, the last words being, "Oh, God!"

Wow! Was I impressed! We were let off the bus at a stop too far on from our usual one, and it seemed the best opportunity to test my new-found words of wisdom...

"Oh, God, Daddy, we've got miles to walk!"

"Don't swear, Karen,"

"Why not?"

"Because it's very, very bad."

Silence...thinking it over...then...

"You swore, Daddy, are you very bad?"

I was nearly marched off my feet as a result, and the pace of our walk suddenly and strongly speeded up!

We always had a budgie flying around the place. Not wise really, as Dad and I were allergic to them, but as kids Sheena and I loved them. Since I was born, successive generations of budgies, all called 'Cheeky', usually yellow, were usually photographed sitting on someone's head — and usually met very nasty ends! One drowned in the washing-up basin, one suffocated down my bed, and one went through the terrible trauma of a broken leg. These fates only occurred now and again. The budgies were loved by us all, in fact, that may have been the problem: certainly in the case of Sheena's budgie, 'Crocky Bird' (don't ask me why she called him that!).

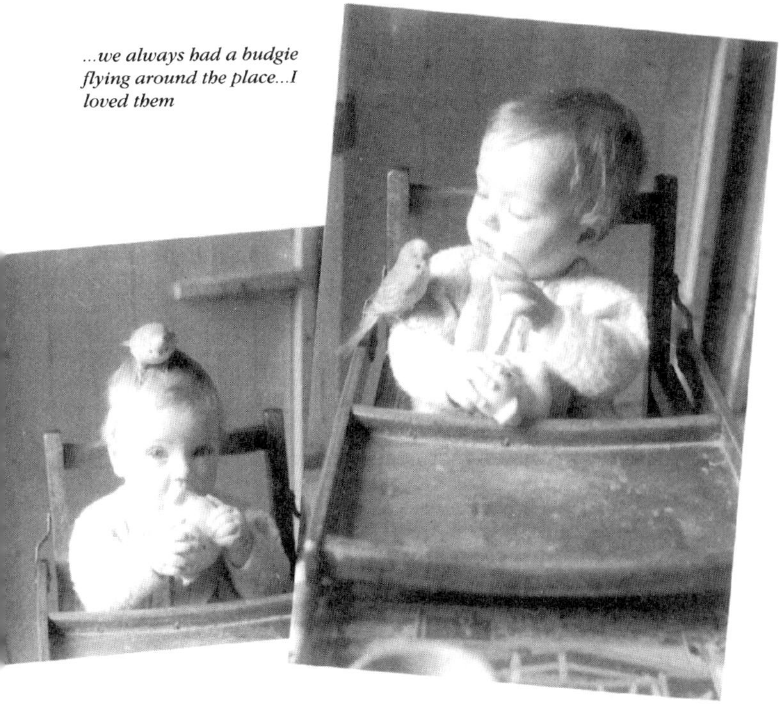

...we always had a budgie flying around the place...I loved them

Anyway, it was my fault, for as I padded off to the kitchen one morning, I slammed the door shut behind me. Poor old Crocky Bird was asleep on top of the door, failed to wake up in time and had his leg broken. There was dismay and hysteria for me, and Dad, Mum and Sheena were woken up: I was aghast at what I'd done and terrified that the bird would die.

It was Dad who had the embarrassing chore of taking poor Crocky Bird to the vet. In fact the budgie went in style, in Dad's concertina box no less! Today I wonder what the vet must have thought, as Roy Williamson of The Corries opened his concertina box — and brought out a budgie!

Crocky Bird survived that encounter only to have the humiliation of a full length plaster cast imprison his leg. He tried his best to peck it off, he learned to fly lopsided with it, and to use it to kick the other bird, Cheeky! Sad to say Crocky did not have a long life, but when he eventually went, full military honours were given at his funeral, complete with daisy chains and a lollypop-stick cross.

The budgies always had a way of escaping at the most inopportune moments. Cheeky, (I forget which one!) flew out of our Stirling Road house into the trees of Lomond Park. Roy was sent to fetch him back. This particular 'Cheeky' was rather perverted, in that he kept doing obscene things to the plastic yellow duckling that I played with in the bath. Knowing the budgies amorous intentions, Roy grabbed my squeaky duck and a child's fishing net, and galloped off outside.

It was not long before a crowd had gathered to watch Roy Williamson of The Corries teeter up a shaky ladder to the top of a tree, calling, "Cheeky-Cheeky!" Even worse, the man appeared to be squeaking a child's plastic duck, swiping at thin air with a fishing net, then swearing his head off — before rushing down the ladder, grabbing it and departing for the next tree, where this 'strange' behaviour was repeated all over again!

It's true, people *have* called us a wee bit eccentric over the years! And yes, believe it or not, Dad did catch that bird: mind you, I think the plastic duck was the real bait!

It was a huge empty cavern of a place, the old warehouse next to Waverley Station. Years later, it would be converted into a large shopping centre, but back then, when I was about nine or so, it was dark, damp, and mysterious. When the fair came with all its shows, it was like a Trinidad carnival. Being enclosed, the noise would ricochet off the distant walls and towering roof; hundreds of people came, all talking and laughing, shouting across to each other, or screaming on the 'Waltzers' as they defied the gravitational pull and spun round and round.

I watched wide eyed and excited. I felt butterflies in my stomach about the anticipated visit to 'The Shows'. Bright lights flashed on and off, dazzling me, as I glanced wildly around. Hooters hooted, I could hear mechanical wailing and wicked laughter from the 'ghost train'. The smell of diesel exhaust fumes, candy floss and fried onions hung heavy in the damp night air.

I hung on tight to Daddy's hand, my sister swinging on his other one. The crowd was thick about us, pushing and shoving in eager haste to try out this and that.

"Now listen, you pair," he squatted down so that his face was at our level. (He had his 'serious' face on, so we knew this was important.)

"It's easy to get lost in here!"

We nodded.

"If you get lost I might find it hard to find you."

We nodded again.

the formal family photograph — Sheena, Mum, me, Dad

"So it's *vitally important* that you do not let go of Daddy's hand. Do you understand?"

Once more we nodded, then jumped up and down as he said, "Right, where will we start?"

There was something really safe about being with Dad. It never occurred to us that other people might be dangerous, wicked or stronger; we were certain he was boss of the world. After all we knew what it was like to be on the erring side and we didn't want to have 'the little talk' Dad reserved for misdemeanours! So we held on to Dad's large strong hands and tried the 'flip the penny', 'roll the ball', 'knock the clowns heads down' side shows. He showed me how to fire the rifles (just as well, as I'd have been likely to hit the crowd), and, when crestfallen that I'd lost, he explained that the barrels may have been bent so the line wasn't all that true!

Sheena and I had hysterical almost 'wet-the-knickers' screaming giggles in the crazy mirrors hall. We laughed at Dad's reflection the most, he was always someone to be loved and respected and therefore looked even more ridiculous than we did, (after all, we knew we could be daft!) But he took it all in good part, and pulled faces and grinned back at us. We'd had to prop ourselves up against the walls to keep from rolling about the floor in endless laughter as Dad did funny pantomime acts in front of the mirrors.

The ghost train took the smile off our faces. Wind blew in our hair and the tunnel's darkness would suddenly be lit up by a shrieking luminous ghost or a red, grinning devil, as our driverless train would shoot round a bend into darkness.

Dad loved the dodgem cars. They frightened me, and I probably felt more isolated because I was in one on my own. Sheena, being too little, went with Dad where he hung onto her in case she was ejected by the crashes. Thump, bang, thump again. Desperately I turned the wheel, only to be rammed again. Dad, enjoying himself, Sheena had the wheel and was out to ram everyone! The blue electric sparks at the top of the wires connecting the dodgems to their power alarmed me, and I was always quite glad when the power was cut and like heavy sullen tortoises the dodgems smoothed smoothly and deliberately to a stop. "Again, again," Sheena would yell. I was happier standing outside as a spectator watching all the ramming and crashing and not being part of it.

We went home exhausted, happy with our treasures of plaster model poodles and short-lived goldfish.

"Dad?"

"Mmm"

"Can we go again?"

"Maybe next year!"

Silence ...then...."Can we go tomorrow?"

"No, I'm on tour tomorrow," he said, and frantically puffed away at his cigarette.

Guy Fawkes, Hallowe'en, guising, bonfires and of course the god of pyrotechnics...Fireworks. Magical events for children of all ages, and Dad was no different. He and my mother stoicly put on astonished or shocked faces at our 'trick or treat' type antics, or yelled in mock fright as we jumped out at them from hidden spots behind doors, wearing our gruesome witches' masks.

The best bonfire was in Jamaica Street in Edinburgh. The wood was piled high almost as tall as a house; everyone added bits to it over the weeks prior to November the 5th. When it was lit the roar and crackle of the flames illuminated the whole street, sparks cascading down like a molten waterfall, or gliding upwards caught on the night breeze, a sharp contrast against the ice-cold silver glint from the stars. The sheer intensity of the heat drove you back from the edge, and the climax to the whole adventure was the fire brigade arriving, sirens wailing and engines revving to put out the flames with silver jet-streams of water. And then we'd make our way

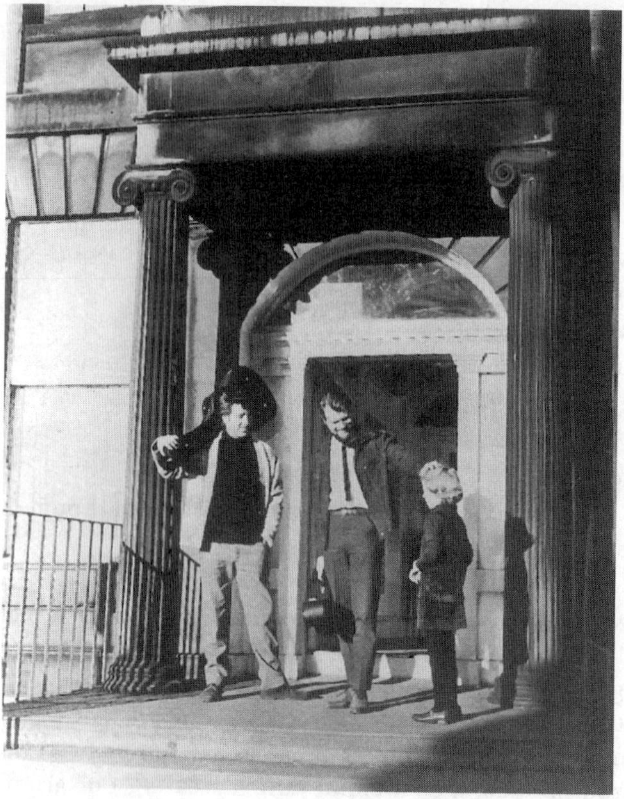

Dad, Ronnie and me in Henderson Row

home, either to watch the firworks being set off in Lomond Park, or even more exciting, to watch Dad set off ours.

He'd have them all lined up in regimental fashion and would lecture us about standing well back.

"I am the only one allowed to handle these," he said.

"Why?"

"Because they can be dangerous."

"How?"

"If you pick one up that's been lit it can explode and burn you,"

"Oooh!!"

"So no touching, right?"

I nodded. Sheena enquired, "Would you be burned right up? And your eyes fall out and insides all get fried?"

With true sisterly concern I told her she was quite right! So we happily allowed Dad the risk of being 'burned right up' instead. The fireworks were wonderful, great explosions of reds, greens, silver and gold. Rockets that whooshed upwards at tremendous speed or sometimes never left the ground, (definite candidates for Dad's dabbling as he tried to find out why, or if the blue touch-paper had been lit); great Catherine wheels and firework fountains.

There was always Magic on November the 5th and to us my father was like some great sorceror wielding inexplicable power over a craft little children could only wonder at. It confirmed the belief of us wee ones that Dad was the law and in charge of Everything!

Because I know the family side of Roy so well, I often wondered what the fans view of him might be. His image on stage was of someone shy but with an undercurrent of laughing good humour, he was musically gifted not just with the ✓ instruments he played, but with his voice, too. A voice that grew richer, better, more harmonious and distinct as the years rolled by. His was the shy reserve to Ronnie's stirring banter or rallying cry to battle.

Perhaps an illusion was created of a pair of country lads, Highland minstrels, down from the mountains to sing their news. Where they lived, what families awaited them, where they were going next was all pretty much left to the imagination. Their mysterious and tireless characters drew vivid fire to the audience's minds: everyone enjoyed The Corries.

And yet sudden, split-second fond memories come to mind of the other side of Roy Williamson. Sprawled in a basket chair, a can of beer in one hand, his eyes glued to the football or rugby action on the black and white television. You could feel the rising tension, hear it in the commentator's voice.

"...and Mac so and so passes to Davies..."

Roy, bolt upright now, can of beer being squeezed to death.

"Daddy, Daddy?"

"...and Roberts evades that, Davies has it..."

"Dad?"

"Not now, Karen," he'd mutter distantly, then he'd growl, "Go on, Davies, get up there!"

"...and Houston takes it from Davies. Was that a foul?..."

"Yes, bloody foul!" Dad would growl.

I would try and watch all those silly wee men with their long baggy shorts down to their knees chasing a ball all over the pitch.

"...The ref's being called in, yes, the ref is going to show a card..."

My eyes switched on to my silent father, as he sat lost in his world of football. Then the wee men were off up the pitch again chasing that ball. I could see him getting tense. The men became very agitated as they neared the goal, then one of them kicked the ball and straight as a die it soared into the net.

"YESS!!!" Roy roared, almost rising to his feet, beer sloshing out of the can. His eyes were alight, as he sat down to watch the next bit of play. For a couple of years I tried to copy him. I'd climb up onto his knee, arms hanging on around his neck and when he roared, I'd roar, though I never really worked out what all the excitement was about. Even the odd stolen sip of beer was totally revolting. One thing I did learn, though, I could ask for anything I wanted just after a 'Roar' and I wouldn't be told off!

Roy wouldn't listen to his own records or watch his own television recordings in public or with us. I'm not sure if it was embarrassment, or the perfectionist in him who, no matter how good a performance, would cringe at the odd bad piece that probably only he alone could detect.

He sometimes took us to a record shop called Rae McIntosh in George Street, Edinburgh. It sold instruments but at the back of the shop was the record department, and while he discussed business with the manager, Sheena and I would nip into one of the listening booths and fight about who was to have the first shot with the heavy earphones. I was always a little embarrassed doing something so conspicuous, but we usually ended happily holding an earphone each, and it was a disappointment when Dad called us away to go home.

...the open road!

At home he was good fun, too.

"Let's have a dance, Karen," he said, grinning at eight year old me.

"I can't dance, Daddy."

"I'll show you how!" he caught my hands in his, and told me to put my right foot on his left one, and my left foot on his right one. Once I was standing on his feet and he'd stopped me falling off by hanging on to my stick-insect arms, he began to waltz silently around the room. It was hilarious. The next trick was holding on to Dad's hands and to do a somersault right through them, by walking up his legs till you spun round. It was like gymnastics for me.

He tried to instill in us a sense of his own philosophies and direction. Protecting us from vanity or showing off was one of his lessons.

"When you meet a friend for the first time, what do you talk about?" he asked us one day.

"Oh, games to play, what we're going to do when we grow up."

"Anything else?"

"Where we go to school and where we live."

"What other things do you talk about?"

"What our parents work at!"

"Ahh. And what do you say about me?"

"Oh," I grinned proudly, "My Daddy is a folk singer, he's in The Corries. They appear on television!"

"Right, Karen: it would be better if you didn't say that,"

"But it's true!"

"Yes, yes, I know it's true, but sometimes it's best not to tell new friends straight away."

I was puzzled and a little offended. I was so proud of my famous Dad. And it had made a huge impact on my friends.

"Why?"

"You can always tell them later, but it's better for the first few visits that your friends like you because of you, not

Californian advertisement

because you've got a daddy on the telly."

"Yes," I said, rather crestfallen and seriously doubting if my friends would be interested in only me!

Looking back on it now I can see the value in Dad's lesson. He was quite right. There are people in this world who latch on to anyone famous as an 'extra string to their bow' just to impress their own friends. And that type of person is the first to drop you in a crisis. Dad was teaching me to find the true value of friendship first, and then at a later date I could divulge the 'secret occupation' of my Daddy.

I saw evidence of this when Mum and Dad divorced. Their

true friends stayed on friendly terms with both of them, but the 'name-droppers' or 'hangers-on' dropped poor Mum like a stone. It hurt her quite a bit as she had done nothing to offend them, and was the same as she had always been. Now I know that she's better off without these people, and Dad had had the canny sense to see straight through them. But his earlier lessons to me were well-founded and something I hold on to to this day.

13

Sheena and I used to get terribly excited about going to the concerts. By now, instead of gigs held in little pubs, The Corries gave solo concerts in the Usher Hall, the King's Theatre and other grand places up and down the country, London and beyond. Gone were the days when they made appearances on other entertainer's shows. Television became more and more accessible to them, through the old black and white recordings of the *White Heather Club, Degrees of Folk,* the 1970 Commonwealth Games, and *The Hoot'nanny Show*, and on to colour filming of The Corries. More records were made.

Sheena and I trotted along to the annual Usher Hall performances with rising excitement and anticipation. Of course we were too young to understand the beauty of the sad slow ballads, but we loved to clap along to the rousing songs.

By about half time, if the truth be told, we would start to get tired and 'girny'. After the fights about who was having a drink of lemonade first, came the real test of strength... the arm wrestle for the only available arm rest. So whilst the haunting strains of one of Ronnie's sad ballads filled the silent listening hall, Sheena and I were locked elbow against bony elbow, shoving for all we were worth! If that didn't work, as soon as the clapping started we dug nails into each other, or kicked each other's ankles, whilst feigning complete indifference. Towards the end of the concert we would become sleepy, but the encores for *The Flower of Scotland* held us spellbound, as the hundreds of hundreds yelled, clapped, stamped, and cheered for more! Finally the lights came on and we made our way backstage. I really loved it (I'm ashamed to admit), as we marched past the long line of fans waiting to meet Dad and Ronnie and have autographs signed. It gave us a small sense of importance, and a huge sense of pride in our Dad.

He was always exhausted after the concerts, and whilst he was changing his clothes and talking with Mum, Sheena and I used to run on to the now empty stage to play. The hall was huge, its very cavernous vastness seemed like the interior of some huge bellied whale. We larked around, pretending to play to an imaginary audience, straining on tiptoes to mouth into the microphones, gleeful if we found one still on!

My memories of my own childhood events are very easily recalled, less so are certain dates, and adults faces that were, to me, distant.

I loved the days when Mum and Dad would take us for picnics, or fishing for minnows at Inverleith pond, or making stone dams at various streams and rivers. They were 'together' days. Very precious, and it felt very right.

Dad was everything to us, he was like a god. Probably because he was away so much, and wasn't always around to tell us off; and then when he did come home he would bring us presents and tell us wonderful stories. There was always great excitement when Dad came home from a tour and gave us his singular attention. But on any odd occasion when he did scold us, one stern word was enough to reduce us to tears.

On the other hand we used to run rings around my mother, and because she was always correcting us we became immune to her rows. I suppose what we really needed, and desperately lacked, was the constant guiding and discipline of a father during our formative years. But then our family was always different! My mother is a very gentle, vague, dreamy sort of a person with many wild, unrealistic thoughts of how the world should be run. She was often interested in analytical, intelligent people who were rather 'high society' in the art world. This enabled Sheena and me to frequently escape her attention, and we were proficient at entertaining ourselves for hours on end.

Children at school used to say how they envied me such a famous life, and I didn't dare admit to them that, for all its glories, I might have swapped it for their seemingly secure family backgrounds; with a 'Dad' coming home every night and helping bring up the kids, and a 'Mum' in a flowery apron, doing home-baking, her life revolving around her children. I dare say my image of their life was as distorted as theirs was of mine.

We were all supposed to move to Stobo, to a little station house in the tiny village, (the railway had been abandoned years beforehand)...but unknown to us, Dad and Mum's marriage had fallen apart, so in the end only Mum, Sheena and I moved to the peace of the Borders. I was now nine years old and Sheena five years younger. We knew no real difference, other than that Dad's tours seemed to take even longer now. But, wow! how we made up for it when he came to visit. Time seemed to pass very slowly when he wasn't here and fly away too quickly when he was.

Stobo made a real impression on me, the little rented station house was a child's dreamland. It stood on its platform with ticket office, waiting room, and outside, the ladies and gents loos! Even the old ticket prices were still printed in gold lettering, on the wall near the waiting room. But it was sad, too, with its railway tracks gone, and whin and gorse bushes growing up between the lines.

The house was pretty, and for once I had my own bedroom. It took hours of academic planning to plaster the walls with the right kind of horse posters! The window looked back along the line to a fringe of whispering, elegant, silver birch trees and, to the south, about half a mile away, the gentle swirl and murmur of the River Tweed.

Many stories of our days at Stobo spring instantly to mind, clamouring like wild children eager to be heard. But I have to be careful to avoid straying from the real purpose of this book, and that has to remain an account of Dad and I, and the effect of his fame on us.

I attended the little local school only two and a half miles away. There were fourteen children in the whole school, and on my birthday everyone was invited back to the station house. Dad couldn't be there on the day but he had popped down for a visit just a few days beforehand. My present had been a wigwam, and after our usual fights, Sheena and I settled down to play in it. Dad wasn't at the birthday party but a nineteen year old girl from Fife came. With long brown hair and big round glasses, she played the guitar, and sang with a pure and strong haunting voice at our little 'get-together'. Barbara Dickson was warm and friendly, and great at entertaining a riot of kids! She wasn't famous then, really more of a friend of the family, but it was not to be long before fame caught her up and swept her along in its whirling torrents, and rushed her to a thrilling life of bright lights, world travel and hectic lifestyles. Roy encouraged her quite a bit, he thought she had a unique and talented singing voice, and she was one of the many guests who appeared on The Corries television shows.

But at my party Barbara Dickson sang for *me,* and I hero-worshipped her! It's a party I'll always remember.

We loved the days Dad came to visit, and would run, elated, out through the front door and down the drive to meet Dad's blue Volkswagen 'Beetle' car. It was an often repeated routine, to jump onto the footguard outside the doors of the car and, hanging on to the open windows, be driven up to the house!

Every moment of those days was treasured, as Dad made up for lost time and spoilt us dreadfully. Before he left for his home, he'd take us for long walks in the countryside. Once, when going through a thick, pine forest I asked him why the trees were only green at the top? And why did they have all those broken branches jutting out at twelve-inch lengths further down?

"Oh, those are for the bears to climb up!"

"BEARS?"

"Yes, there are huge bears in this wood and ... sometimes they're up in the trees watching you!"

He was probably trying to discourage us from wandering or exploring too far on our own, but for years afterwards when I roamed about, I kept looking over my shoulder for angry, giant bears, and convinced all my schoolfriiends likewise!

Horse daft as ever, the highlights of Dad's visits for me were the times he took us to see Sultan, the old brown horse, and the donkey who shared his field. We always brought a whole box of sugar-lumps for them to feast on. Their velvet-covered lips would carefully pluck the sugar-lumps from our trembling, eager hands. Probably the owner would have been horrified at the ill health it could have caused the animals, but as children, we only knew it was what horses liked to eat!

The McCalmans' visited and I remember going searching for conkers with one of them. Many of the famous people who drifted past us are too numerous to call to memory, and to my child-like mind, were just the same as ordinary people.

Whether it was the beautiful countryside or peaceful way of life I'm not sure, but suddenly I was writing poetry, and was astonished to find that Dad was very enthusiastic about it. Well, I was all for 'happy times' and turned it out in my ten year old scrawl. Dad put music to one of my poems, and he and Ronnie sang it on stage. Pride collided with embarrassment in my emotions, and I was moved almost to tears when Dad announced to the huge audience that his eldest daughter had written the next song. Lights dimmed and the soft, rosy spotlights shone down as Dad started picking clear, harplike notes from his guitar as he and Ronnie launched into the serene and somewhat sad song. At the end, the theatre fairly shook with the clapping and cheering, of course it was for Roy and Ronnie, but deep in my heart I was elated that part of it might be for my poem!! I was a real bore about it for weeks afterwards.

The days at Stobo passed as Summer sped into Autumn. The Tweed overflowed its banks with the downpour of storms, and became a raging, wild, brown fury, ripping two-hundred year old trees from the hillside, and flying them along in its earbursting roar. And as quickly it was gone, leaving shallow pools on the fields around. When these froze over, Sheena and I slid and skated on them, in our wellies, and had even bigger and better battles for hours on end.

One night I remember Mum waking us, wrapping us up in cloaks, and leading us out into the pitch dark night. Gradually our eyes grew accustomed to the dim glow from the thousands of stars up above. Speaking softly she told us the night was full of life, and if we listened we would hear it. The three of us stood there under the stars, lost in the huge expanse of night-time. Owls hooted, bats flitted and whirred overhead, occasionally uttering a squeak, and all about us little furry creatures scurried, or rustled in the whins on their nocturnal hunts. Distantly deer barked, and nearer at hand the 'yip, yip' of a fox, or the scream of a rabbit. I felt very small, dwarfed by it all. I had always believed that when I went to bed, so did the rest of the world. Hundreds of questions tumbled in my mind, but I was too awestruck to speak of them then.

In the days that followed, I became very aware of my wild environment. I would wander for miles, with or without Sheena, eating wild raspberries, blackberries, thistle flowers soft kernels, rosehips. It was a carefree time of learning and exploring, and climbing silver birch trees to watch the hundreds of ants scrambling around with earnest intent, like harassed London businessmen. We collected fish and tadpoles (and inadvertently killed a few with our ignorance) and admired caterpillars and butterflies, birds and beasts, and as always waited like mad for Dad to visit again.

George Weir was a very serious man, and yet he could be

humorous too. He loved history with a great intensity and enthusiasm, especially...history of the time of Robert the Bruce. He used to drive our baker's van, (George, not Robert the Bruce!) On his rounds from Peebles, George would always stop at our house for at least two hours! He could make history come alive, and Sheena and I would sit enthralled, eating freshly-made pink-iced buns, whilst all around us Robert the Bruce fought bloodthirsty battles and rode magnificent horses. I'm not sure if it was George who told me about the horses or if it was my imagination flaring with as much fervour as his!

George had a real gift for writing verse around his favourite subjects. Many of these Roy eventually made into songs, such

Roy, George Weir and Ronnie

as *Liberty, Lord Yester, The Heidless Cross,* and others like *Weep ye Weel by Atholl, Flodgarry, The Black Douglas, and Arkinholm*, and they became well known as part of The Corries collection of ballads and fighting legends.

Roy was fond of George and we often went to visit him, when George would play a verse or two on the 'plank' as he called his home-made guitar. On George's birthday, Dad and I played a typical Williamson practical joke! We bought a beatiful little golden clock, and then hid it in the centre of a loaf of bread. The original wrapping was carefully put back on, and then the whole thing was put in a box and gift-wrapped. Poor George must have thought we were off our heads gift-wrapping what appeared to be just a loaf of bread. He did eventually discover the clock!

It was with fearful heartbreak that we left Stobo to go back to Edinburgh to live. Mum had done her best to excite us about returning to the city, but I was sad to leave the paradise I had found, and perhaps the only place where I could have kept a pony.

Finbar Furey from Ireland, and his wife Sheila, moved into the station house after us, and it was nice to know the house was occupied by a friend we knew, rather than by strangers. Dad had been Finbar's Best Man at his wedding.

Finbar and his brothers of course were to become famous as one of Ireland's best known folk groups, The Fureys. They came to Edinburgh as young lads with an interest in folk music, around 1966, and played at the 1967 Edinburgh Festival. Originally from Ballyfermot, Ireland, they brought with them a wild mystical Irish sound in their music, and took Scotland by storm. Ted Furey, their father, was a well-respected musician in his own right and the boys inherited his talent. Finbar was 'All Ireland Champion Piper' at the age of only fourteen. Many other major prizes came his way, so it was hardly surprising they developed a huge following in Scotland, both countries sharing a natural love of Celtic sounds.

Roy always had a high regard for the Fureys, and often went to visit them, to chat or discuss some new sound in music with them. They, too, sometimes popped down to our house, but, sadly for me now, they were just faces in a crowd of the many grown-ups who visited us. I was too young to appreciate fully the music, but I'll always remember Finbar and Eddie's wonderful Irish accents, they had a lilting drowsy way of speaking, lit up here and there with an infectious burst of quiet laughter.

It was Finbar Furey who taught Roy so much about the flute, he never forgot that and often spoke of Finbar's craftmanship. Roy was a brilliant flute-player, but Finbar was the king! Eddie Furey wrote a lot of the songs they sing, but it's

Roy (left) was Best Man at Finbar Furey's wedding with Sheila Peebles in 1968 (actress Alison Peebles on the right)

his unusual, gravelly rough Irish tones that bring images of dark crofts, and bright hearts, deep in emerald country. It speaks of the sad and harsh environment caught up with the beautiful, and the purity of an ancient way of life. He has been compared to the famous Luke Kelly who used to play in The Dubliners, but I think Eddie's voice has a subtle difference. I feel also that first and foremost the Fureys play the music they love, the music that lies deep within their souls, they are not playing merely just to entertain.

I will never forget Finbar cutting short a hectic, pressurised tour to fly over to be with us at Dad's funeral, and his offer to play an Irish lament on the pipes for Dad, it brings tears to my eyes now, years later, and I know Dad would have been proud and touched that Finbar would do this.

14

Edinburgh was dismal, after the freedom I had known, and we were somewhat cramped, moving in to my grandparents' council flat. The best consolation was the close contact with Granny, Mum's mother. She was a wonderful woman, small in stature, but a giant in warmth and love for us all. Her affection surrounded us in a homely world of care and security. Tucking us up in bed at night, looking after us during the day, taking us for walks, telling us stories, or making us 'cocoa-and-toast'. Granny filled the part that, in me, wanted a *display* of love, and she did, I daresay, spoil us dreadfully.

outside my grandparents flat in Edinburgh; Dad visiting Sheena (left) and me

Grandad could be fun too, taking us to the canal to walk along the old tow-path, or sticking some of my model horses onto an old wheel on its side, so when you spun the wheel the horses galloped round and round. He loved to tell us ghost stories, or tales from his past, but he also liked to tease us, or argue for the last word, of course all done in fun, but it really used to infuriate me! Looking back it taught me a lot about patience with other folk, and it served to educate me, as I was somewhat lacking contact with people on a one-to-one basis.

Dad used to visit us quite often, and he loved playing music with Grandad, the two would sit having a quiet drink, and Dad would play his guitar or whistle, whilst Grandad cheerily belted away on his beautiful accordion. Christmas was always good fun, Dad trying to sneak our presents in without us seeing him. By now, I had realised Santa Claus was a myth, but I was in no hurry to grow up, 'Grown-ups' never seemed to have much fun.

Dad made a dream come true for me one day when he told me I could have riding lessons at a nearby stables. I was almost sick with excitement, the butterflies were doing 'loop-the loops' in my tummy! I was on such a high each time he drove me to the stables, that I'm sure I must have been truly unbearable. I was so proud that I wore my new riding hat everywhere I went (I'd have worn it to bed, had it not been so uncomfortable!). Dad was visibly horrified by this and wondered if perhaps I was slightly insane! He was most embarrassed once, when he stopped the car outside a newsagent, and sent me in to buy him a packet of cigarettes, I rushed in wearing my riding hat, and a pair of pink-and-white shorts! But the real truth was that I was just a kid, eager to tell the world I loved horses and now was riding them.

Dad was very good about taking me to the stables, but just occasionally he'd let me down. I'd be sitting at the window, silent and tense, chanting over and over, "I'll be good, I'll be really good, just let Dad come." I'd peer into the distance, desperate to catch a glimpse of the car, almost cold-sweating as the clock inched nearer to the time the ride would set off without me. And when the clock chimed...a huge, engulfing wave of despair washed and smothered me. I'd be depressed for days, until the weekend drew nearer again, bringing the time for my riding lesson once more.

Dad and I grew closer. He took us swimming at the Commonwealth Pool, and almost succeeded in teaching me to overcome my fear of the water. He was good with us, made us laugh and encouraged us to overcome little failures.

Being a father to us can't have been altogether easy, especially when Sheena and I persuaded him to take us to see the film *Paint Your Wagon* no less than six times (— no wonder he kept singing *Wandering Star* wherever we went!) and how Sheena got him to go and see *Tales of Beatrix Potter* (ballet at that!), I'll never know, but full marks to Dad for sitting it out. At the end of one film we went to, the pleading voice of Sheena said, "I need to go to the toilet!"

"Can't you hang on, love?" he whispered back.

Ronnie and Roy with fans from south of the Border

"No, I need *now,*" she said challengingly. At that moment the National Anthem boomed across the loudspeakers (that was before they knew Dad had written a Scottish one!). The entire audience rose respectfully to its feet. Sheena looked round in wonderment, and asked, "Why is everyone standing up?" Quick as a flash I answered,"Because they all need the loo, too!" Wow, was she worried!

After the cinema, came the Chinese meal. It was a well loved routine for all of us. In between beansprouts, cashew nuts, and special fried chicken, Dad would tell us funny stories, or try to educate us in some topic or another. Little by little he was stretching our minds, and we rose eagerly to his guidance, keen to please. Sometimes though, we'd notice he was tired or depressed, and he didn't really want us there. I think his unyielding sense of duty made him carry on, when probably he could have done with catching up on a few hours sleep at home. Perhaps the loyalty he gave us was a way of overcoming the lack he felt his own parents had displayed towards him.

He would keep us spellbound, or hysterical with laughter at some of the tour-time tales he had accumulated. Anyone who has ever spoken to Roy Williamson will realise that his stories were all the more funny for the way in which he described things, and his ability to re-enact various conversations or self-doubting thoughts.

When out on stage in front of a huge crowd, for sheer devilment during a sad song, and usually when Dad was playing a haunting lament on the flute, he would turn to Ronnie, and very slowly defy Ronnie to laugh, as his eyes gradually became cross-eyed! The Corries were always playing practical jokes on each other, and now and again the audience were involved, too.

On one April Fool's day, Dad and Ronnie dressed up two of the sound recordists in The Corrie clothes, and sent them on to the waiting stage. It was the Usher Hall, Edinburgh, and the crowd roared and cheered a welcome to the two red-shirted figures that could only be The Corries! Struck dumb with instant stage fright, the two men stared aghast at the yawning cavern reaching endlessly in front of them, filled from top to bottom with howling, cheering, stamping hordes! One of them spoke nervously into the mike...:

"April Fool," and the crowd began to suspect something was up — that 'Roy' seemed to have put on a bit more bulk and 'Ronnie' lost a little height; the clapping started to slow and become hesitant. People coughed nervously, not sure what this was all about? Where were Roy and Ronnie? Had someone kidnapped them? Did these two substitutes think they could dare replace the music the crowd had come to hear?!

It was all too much for the sound engineers...nervously they backed off that stage and belted to the dressing rooms, and a long cool pint of much needed beer — and Roy and Ronnie burst onto the stage strumming guitars and teasing the crowd,

"Ha, ha, ha, we got you! April Fool!"

The crowd loved the cheek of it, it put them in fine fettle for the rest of the show. Later the two sound engineers said that walking on to that stage was one of the most frightening things they had ever had to do!

On more than one occasion at concerts the practical jokes of The Corries backfired on them; as Dad himself describes so well in a letter to me written in 1976:

Aberdeen

Dear Karen,

Well, here we are in Aberdeen. Rain — rain — rain & more rain!

...Both Ronnie & I have had the flu. He in fact collapsed on stage in Dunfermline three songs into the second half and I had to carry him off.

Streuth what a weight! The audience thought that it was one of our jokes and laughed heartily. When I came back on to explain what happened there were cries of "Oh yes, what's the punchline?" They couldn't believe that 'big strong Ron' had melted. However they were very sympathetic in the end.

....Sorry for the dreadful scribble but I'm still feeling a bit limp, full of aspirin, etc. "Excuses — excuses!" says you, "Own up, Dad — you're just a lousy writer!"

THAT'S ALL FOR NOW
love from
Dad x x x x x x x

On another occasion it was Dad who collapsed on stage in horrific pain (I think it was a gallstone). Ronnie anxiously yelled out to the crowd,

"Is there a doctor in the house?"

The crowd burst into laughter, and applauded him! He had

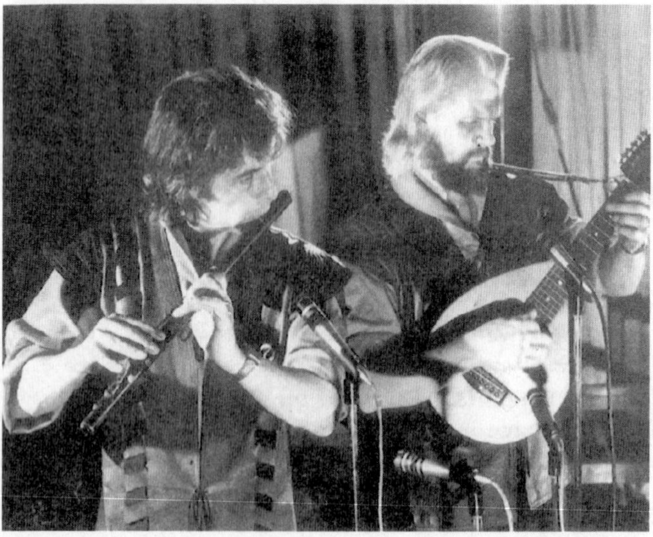

photo: Graham Falconer

in concert

to keep asking and telling them it wasn't a joke before they finally believed him.

(In fact even due to illness The Corries very, very rarely postponed concerts.)

At one cinema, in Edinburgh I believe, there used to be a heavy safety fire curtain. This would descend to the floor, and then six feet deeper, into a specially cut trench. At one performance, I think it was Dad who, having sung the last encore, was walking backwards, waving and bowing to the crowd, and failed to take the safe route Ronnie had taken. He waved one final time, went behind a light stage curtain, and promptly fell down the six foot gap! He was lucky not to have broken a leg, but the way Dad told us and how he re-enacted the professional smooth exit with the daft fall, had us grinning for ages.

Occasionally, other external unexpected 'UFOs' appeared. Singing a sad ballad, with the lighting subdued and the crowd silently listening, absorbing the atmosphere, things were totally ruined when the cinema's huge, fat cat purposefully, yet sedately, minced across the stage from one side to the other. I think Dad said the crowd practically gave it a standing ovation!

At one Edinburgh theatre, Dad and Ronnie gave their usual brilliant performance, but marred by one thing. The spotlights. They went on at all the wrong times, or slowly shifted off Dad, in such a manner that the audience would not have seen him at all if he had not to a certain extent 'waltzed' with the fidgeting spot of light. I asked him backstage what had gone wrong. He smiled, and said he was not all that sure, but it may have had something to do with him falling out with the lighting man!

On the whole most people got on well with Roy Williamson, he was always keen to help those who were trying to help themselves. But his discipline could be strict and unyielding, (and I knew full well what being on the other side of his temper was like!) Luckily, that side of him was fairly well-controlled and scarcely seen.

His contacts never failed to amaze me, he knew people from all walks of life, from all over the world. When the entire van-load of Corries instruments was stolen, including his much loved and irreplaceable Combolins, the police tried their best, but failed to unearth the missing instruments. But within twenty-four hours the instruments had been located through contacts of Dad's, and the show could go on. Only two instruments were missing, probably sold abroad.

15

'Adventures' were looked forward to with great anticipation by Sheena and I. They were always a mystery, and Dad wouldn't drop any clues where we were going till we got there. You could tell that he did most of the organising, because most of the time the excursions led to the harbour, or the beach. I can still feel the excitement and wonder that those trips held for us, and the contented feeling that we were with our 'Daddy', the person who could make problems disappear, and dreams come true. Of course Dad wasn't such a god, he was a normal human being with normal failings, but to our young minds he was everything: he was *Dad!*

In his spare time he liked to go fishing, and on one particular occasion, decided to teach me the sport. I felt so proud, as he taught me how to set up a rod, how to rub the ends of the pole segments in your hair, so that the natural oil would prevent the pole jamming and thereby making it more difficult to dismantle. There was a special knot to tie the cat gut to the line. I've never forgotten it! Dad would then move upstream to fish in peace, whilst I inexpertly creamed the water to a lather downstream, using my rod like a circus-master's whip. Incredibly, I actually caught one, but was so full of anguish for it, that I unhooked it and let it go. I'm still not sure if Dad believed me or not!

After fishing, we went exploring and found an old ruined castle, high up on a steep bank. The Borders of Scotland are full of such ruins. Dad climbed up its treacherously loose stonework to explore, and called down to me descriptions of all he could see. Then driving back to the 'Black Bull' at Lauder, he'd fill my imagination with stories of people who might have lived in the castle, and the battles they might have fought. It was so exciting being with Dad on holiday, just the two of us. I decided to be 'adult' in my behaviour as much as possible, and make him proud of me; it worked most of the time, but I tended to ask too many questions which would tire him out. Word soon got round the little hotel that here was Roy Williamson of The Corries and I felt really awed when a crowd gathered round us in the lounge one evening to watch Dad and I play chess. Actually I was only learning the game, and Dad always played fairly in that although he always won, it was seemingly only at the last possible moment, so that I was always encouraged to try to beat him next time.

One sunny day Dad really excelled himself in his endurance of children, and took not only his two daughters, but also our young cousin Sean to Edinburgh zoo. He wasn't just being dutiful, he really did seem to enjoy taking us round the animals, (although he was desperate to have a smoke!) Pictures spring to mind, Dad in his flared corduroy trousers, white t-shirt, long hair and sideburns. Sheena perched high on his shoulders, Sean galloping along frightening passers-by with an imitation rubber snake, and me running knock-kneed and gangling.

My sister and I had moved with Mum to a house in Dean Village (still part of Edinburgh), and I went to Flora Stevenson's school just down the road. Dad still came to visit us, but by now I knew that it was more than fame that was keeping him away. Mum had new friends now, I liked some of them, whilst others seemed false and overly friendly to me, one even told me he was my 'Uncle Paddy'. Dad, too, introduced us to his new girlfriends, all of them seemed to me to be nice, although I remember thinking that it was such a shame none of them owned a horse!

The concerts were still great fun, and Dad took us down to Stirling Road for meals quite often, it was still our real home with the warmth of memories lingering there.

After a long while at Dean Village, we moved to Learmonth Grove (which wasn't all that far away really). I met Granny Williamson (Dad's mother) again, she was very tall and seemed to me to have no sense of humour, by now she was a little eccentric to say the least! However, she got on very well with Mum, and fascinated the pair of us. 'Victorian' is the word that really summed her up. We had tea with her in the North British Hotel on Princes Street, where she caused quite a stir, and later she made us get down on our backs in Princes Street Gardens to do 'Keep Fit' exercises. People walking past must have thought we were some kind of pre-Festival display, but there was no arguing with Granny Williamson. Yet for all her strange notions and lack of humour, she was generous too, and I still have the engagement ring that she gave to me. It must have meant a great deal, it was beautifully inscribed by my grandfather, and had a pretty array of emeralds and

photo: Graham Falconer *Roy and Ronnie*

garnets. By her very unpredictability and regal manner I remember her vividly with love, and a little fear.

Dad drove a different Volkswagen now, it was still blue and still a 'Beetle' model, but Sheena and I missed the little sunroof the old one had. Both of us used to stand up on the car seats, leaning half out through the opening, singing *Three Wheels On My Wagon* at the tops of our voices, and with a laugh, Dad joined in too. We had a wonderfully harmomious rendition of *Cookaburra Sits In The Old Gum Tree,* and, over the cobble stones and potholes, not quite so harmonious! One day when driving on one of our 'Adventures', we drove, quite by chance, up behind the *old* Volkswagen Beetle. Dad was amused by this and we followed the old car for miles. It must have looked strange, two blue cars of the same make, chasing each other, especially when the one in front started to become alarmed and began evasive tactics, with sharp turns!

Mum couldn't look after me one morning, so Dad took me with him to the BBC recording studios. Of course being me, I soon became bored. Overall images that I can recall were a disappointment that the entire studio was not lit up, like some palace, that in fact it was a fairly drab place, except where the cameras were pointed. Lots of scaffolding, people and TV cameras. Only the set was bright and clean, I had thought the whole place would have been some kind of glamour world. Most likely I was a pest as well as a constant liability, so I was given a 'Kit-Kat' to eat, and a ride on Camera 3 (that's the one like a crane, that can go really high for angled shots from above). It was like sitting in a lift.

Somewhere about this time Mum met Igor Baranov. He was a huge man with a definite weight problem, and I did not like him. My world took a downward plunge of despair as Mum, Sheena and I travelled to London to live. I thought it was only for a holiday, but the days stretched on and on. My beloved riding lessons were lost, my friends all gone, and no physical contact with Dad or Granny. But children are adaptable, and I tried. Poor Igor, he loved Mum, treated Sheena as a little doll to dress up and show off, but could not cope with me as I started to reach my difficult twelfth year. I rebelled against him, and he must have hated me for it. On the whole we were an inconvenience to him, and I had a very unhappy time down in London. I suppose I never gave him much of a chance, and probably saw him subconciously as a threat to Dad. Sheena and I were often dragged along, feeling car-sick, in his Ford Mustang, and when left on our own, we went through every I-spy, Alphabet and Spot the Car games we knew, but invariably we'd end up fighting.

On one occasion, Igor got so mad at us moaning, that he shouted at us before disappearing into the pub. It was then I suppose my frustration blew its top. I was downcast at being in such a huge polluted city, with no green fields, and depressed at never being able to do right or be valued. I tried to set fire to Igor's car whilst we were in it. Well, I never could get things right, and luckily for me this daft plan backfired. The underside of Igor's car seats melted instead of burned. Igor apparently never noticed, and as it was his business to sell cars the Ford Mustang was exchanged soon afterwards.

One day, we were told that Dad was coming to visit. Sheena and I were almost ill with excitement. We hadn't seen him for so long! The weather was awful, but neither of us noticed, to us it seemed the best and brightest of days.

Dad took us out for a meal and then a trip to Madame Tussaud's waxworks museum, which was very interesting, if somewhat unnerving! all those upright wax bodies, silent and sneering. We walked back to the car as the evening was descending, and the street lights blinked suddenly to life. The hustle and bustle of the working day was over, and the shops were closed. The three of us paused at one huge window, began to smile, and then to laugh. The dummies stood stern, not amused, slightly pompous..and entirely naked! Even more comical, one of the dummies had toppled over, and now lay, in a state of arrogant *rigor-mortis,* legs in the air. Not only naked but bald as well. Sheena and I laughed until the tears ran down our faces and our jaws ached. I think it did us all good that day, it certainly eased the frustration building up in me.

I'm not sure if Dad and Mum had a talk about me, or if any particularly searching questions were asked. But not long after, when Dad was back in Edinburgh he phoned Mum, and after speaking with him, she passed the phone to me.

"Hi, Dad!"

"Hi, love, how's it going?"

"Oh, okay," (my standard reply.)

"How would you like to come back up here to live?"

I was stunned, my heart thumped wildly, "Oh Dad, could I?"

"And something else, Karen..."

"Yes?"

"I've bought you a horse."

There was an excited moment of silence, whilst my memory played over his words again and again and again.

"You still there?" he asked, the line crackling long distance.

"Oh, Dad, is it true?" I wanted to burst into tears, and didn't understand why good news should make me feel that way! Then like the flood gates rustily creaking open, my thoughts tumbled into racing speech.

"What's it like? How old is it? A pony or a horse? What's its name? Where is it now?...How soon can I see it?"

What a transformation in my life. All of a sudden, I owned a half share in a horse, with a girl called Maureen Turnbull. I was sent to boarding school, and in the holidays lived with my mother's parents. Like a breath of fresh air, green fields were available to me once more, both at school and with Pharoah, my horse. The arrangement with the horse worked really well, I owned him during school holidays and days off, and Maureen had him the rest of the time.

Dad told me years later that the hardest part for him was when he left me standing waving goodbye on the front steps of my new school...Oxenfoord, in Edinburgh, (which closed down this year, 1993). He said he almost turned the car around to come back and take me away! I'm very glad he didn't. Oxenfoord was the making of me in the same way Gordonstoun had been the making of him. I loved my time there. Oh, yes, there were moments of homesickness, but I was so horse-daft that really I filled my time with dreams of horses! I made quite a few friends at Oxenfoord, and it was great fun when we were all taken on outings. On one such occasion, I went to a play at the Little Lyceum in Edinburgh. To my amazement, Dad and Ronnie were playing next door, so at half time I rushed next door, with a hastily scrawled note, scribbled on paper torn out of an exercise book.

> Dear Dad,
>
> I am just next door, we are seeing a play, so I thought I'd write you a note! Good luck with the concert.
>
> Lots of love.
>
> Karen.

I gave the note to Lee Elliot, (who helped manage The Corries), as Roy and Ronnie were on stage, and then I rushed back, scared I'd miss the rest of the play and possibly the bus back to school.

The headmistress was great, and used to let me stay up to watch Dad on television, although the other girls used to get bored, they didn't understand Folk Music, and would have preferred staying up to listen to the charts! I didn't see so much of Dad whilst I was at school, and the holidays tended to clash with The Corries tour time. But he wrote often, and phoned, and sent books, etc. His letters always made me smile with their funny cartoons at the bottom of a page. Now and again I was allowed a day out from school. Dad would pick me up, and run me to my horse, and afterwards he'd take me home to Stirling Road, where he'd cook us both a meal. He was certainly no cook, but then I wasn't either, so his 'beans on toast' were bliss to me!

Dad loved mountaineering (he had been in the Outward Bound School in his younger days), and he encouraged this interest in me, too. When all my fellow classmates were reading *Jackie* magazines in their free time, I was scaling impossible heights and dangerous blizzards through the pages of a copy of *Everest The Hard Way,* or of *Annapurna,* that he had lent me. He really opened my eyes to adventure, and to other countries. I think I had a schoolgirl crush on Dougal Haston, when all my friends were screaming for Donny Osmond. I began to thirst for adventure and excitement, and loved films on such subjects. Dad's fascination with science fiction and astronomy fairly kept me spellbound; soon our conversations naturally became extended, as we were both enthused with the same subjects. As he wrote,

> ...By the way could you phone *urgently* next term's half-holiday dates as we are making up our tour list on Fri.

one of Dad's cartoon's from a letter to me

... Glad you liked *Everest;* I haven't read it yet so don't lose it!! or else.

see you soon
lots of love
Dad xxxxxx

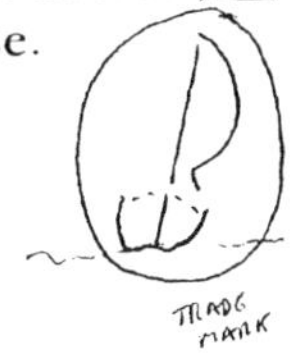

He painted a little seascape for me (it was during the time he was experimenting with acrylic paints). It was a pretty little scene, a square-rigger fighting a swelling sea. It was on a sheet of primed hardboard, and I kept it on show, above the mantelpiece in the dormitory. Regrettably, during an 'inter-gang' pillow fight, it was knocked down a crack in the back of the mantelpiece, where it has remained ever since. Perhaps in years to come it will be discovered, and people will wonder how it got there.

Mum and Sheena moved back to Granny's from London, things not having worked out there. I was glad to see them back. Sheena went to a local day school; we moved out of Granny's, to a nearby house that Dad had bought for us in Calder Road, and he visited us quite often there.

One Christmas Day he came round and played the guitar. We all sang carols, and as my Christmas present had been a tape-recorder, I recorded the afternoon. It's a tape I still have and treasure. I suppose it was the nearest to my ideal of a normal family Christmas. Dad was playing all sorts of 'twiddly' classical pieces on the guitar, interspersed with wild bursts of Flamenco, or very fast tunes on the penny whistle. I, desperate to please, asking all sorts of questions, in my teenage boarding school accent. Sheena had the giggles, and Mum can be heard yelling from the kitchen... "Sheena, did you eat two pounds of tomatoes out of this fridge?" whilst Sheena's new Christmas present...a cat, crept behind the arm-chair (Dad's one)...to throw up hairballs and other unmentionables. Just a normal family Christmas!

16

For a while my father became intrigued, and to a certain degree angered, by our country's politics. He believed passionately in the Scottish National Party, yet was furious about the lack of support for this young independance group. He wasn't the only one, a lot of Scottish people were beginning to awaken to the way they had been seemingly forgotten as the 'far away' tip of the British Isles! Dad loved to debate the pros and cons of each argument, and he took an interest in the discussions on television. Having said all that however, he became disillusioned about the SNP's hopes of success, not through any fault of that party, but because the odds from south of the border (to his mind) seemed so overwhelming. He believed the SNP was one of the best parties at keeping in touch with people at all levels, right down to the grass roots, and it was this awareness of the people as a whole, he felt, that could make Scotland a better place.

Once when the recession was hitting everyone badly, Dad filled the loft at home with enormous quantities of bulk buying. The more popular items of course we went through fairly rapidly, but I'll always remember we had enough tins of beans to see us to the moon and back. And where he got all those boring bars of green soap, I couldn't begin to imagine.

One of his bulk stores made him dangerously ill. It was during the days when he was still on the old style of asthma inhaler, the one with a soft bulb that you squeezed. This in turn sent the liquid up through a tiny pipe, turning it into spray which you then inhaled. I think, if memory serves me correctly, that Dad had heard the ingredients were about to be taken off the market and replaced with something else.

Knowing that he was shortly to go away on tour, he did not want to have side-effects from any new type of asthma inhaler affecting how he performed on stage. He went to his doctor and told a huge fib! He explained he was off to climb mountains abroad with a team, and they would be away from civilisation for most of a year, therefore it was important he take all medication with him, and he asked for a bulk load of the little vials that fed the inhaler. The doctor was understandably very reluctant to comply: the liquid was poisonous if taken above the amounts dictated. But Dad was persuasive.

He was happy with his long-term supply and did not abuse the instructions. Unfortunately, many months later, he began to experience horrific headaches, blacking out and nausea and dizziness. No one could understand what was wrong, he went from doctors to specialists; and then one day he phoned me at school to tell me the verdict on all these tests...***A suspected brain tumour***.

He was anxious and depressed, as were we all. There were more tests to be done. The old inhaler by now had long been taken off the market, and it was just by chance that the doctors discovered that Dad was still using his. A new test was sought, a new verdict obtained: he had poisoned himself with the old medicine by forgetting that it had a short shelf life. The ingredients had changed to a lethal concoction, and he was lucky he had not killed himself! A switch to the new Ventolin inhaler, and his 'brain tumour' disappeared! (As did bulk-buying for a while).

Sheena and I were growing up now, although still fighting...we were very much sisters. Sheena came to Oxenfoord when she was twelve, but only stayed one and a half terms. In many ways her insecurity came to the fore there, whereas mine seemed to vanish. 'Chalk and Cheese', my Aunt used to call us because of our differences!

Here is an extract from a letter Dad wrote to me at this time,

> ...Karen, you may notice from the post-board that

I'm writing rather more to Sheena than you at the moment. Don't take offence! It's just that in the few moments between work that I have for letter writing I feel that perhaps she needs the communication more. It's good to hear, though, that she's settling down a bit better.

Hey! I really liked one of your 'scribbles' (as you call them) in your last letter; the one of the horse, looking at it from the side, cantering past, very flowing, if you see what I mean. Terrific.

He began to drill me into working hard for my 'O' level exams. The extra attention was pleasing, and I loved all his stories of his own schooldays:

Zetland Place

Dear Karen

Just got back from the far North and got your letter. ...

... Sounds like fun, the electricity going off, it reminds me of my early school days away up in Aberlour. Our 'dump' was lit by carbide gas and occasionally there would be an air bubble in the supply so all the lights would go out, but the gas still continued to come ut of the burners so we couldn't even have candles and had to creep about with torch batteries. (This was not in the days before electricity was invented! I'm not *that* old.) It was just that we were so far from a supply.

Enclosed, by the way, is a special 'magic' pen for passing exams. (hint! hint!)

... Well, we only just made it back from Orkney (I hope you got my P.C.) It was blowing a force 11 gale, gale forces only go up to 12 on the Beaufort scale, so you can imagine it was pretty rough. I'm sure you'd have enjoyed it!

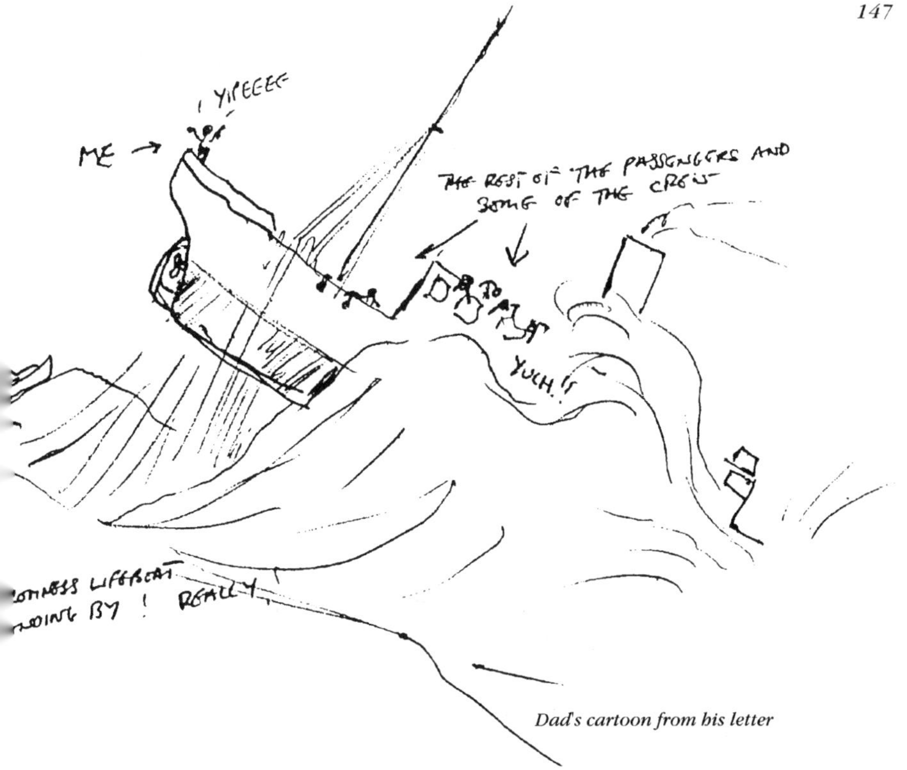

Dad's cartoon from his letter

We had fun too! I remember he took me camping once...it was a total disaster. We pitched the tent under some tall trees, near a burn that flowed into a nearby loch. The 'Intrepid explorers' then set out for a walk, right round the loch. It was really miles, and we got lost. (I know, how can anyone get lost walking in a circle, sooner or later you're bound to end up back at the start!) When we did find the tent again, we were exhausted.

No sooner were we inside, than it poured with rain, pelting down like painful slingshots: Dad and I cowered in the tent, and listened to it rattling outside. Darkness came, and the wind grew strong. Still it rained. I needed the loo, and Dad, (so used to coping for himself) had nevertheless forgotten one important necessity...the loo roll! Out I tottered, into the howling gale, with my calor gas lamp, and three pages ripped from Dad's favourite book!

Sleep that night was nearly impossible, and eventually Dad told me in a loud voice (to make himself heard over the storm outside), that we had to get out of the tent and sleep in the car. Tree-roots moved like giant animal fingers beneath my sleeping bag, and the little trickling stream outside was now a raging force that had burst its banks and was inching ever closer to the little tent. The huge old pine trees were drunkenly swaying, and it was their roots that now began to lift the tent.

Poor Dad, he had to sleep behind the wheel of the car all night, as I snored on the back seat, the car itself shuddering in the wind. Like most children I was totally confident that no harm would come to us, because Dad was there.

Roy in the early 1960s *photo: Graham Falconer*

My mother had an ability to make the best of a bad situation, and these little episodes coloured the early years of my sister and I. And now I realise that what we lacked in conventional material belongings, we more than made up in 'adventures'. I know it has given me the knowledge that no matter what the problem, there is a way round it, you've just got to look, and sometimes in the most unexpected ways. Sometimes I get frustrated by people giving up as soon as a few problems come up in their lives. But then, 'Nowt as queer as folk'.

I suppose surrounded by conventional kids with conventional parents, I was acutely aware of the difference in mine, When you're a kid it's vital to be part of the peer-group herd, or so you think, and whereas Dad's unusual work and hobbies and ideas were held in much esteem by others and their parents because Dad was famous, Mum had no such title and her breaks with convention in many ways were labelled eccentric. I was always telling my friends they didn't understand, and yet always telling Mum she didn't understand. I was an awful teenager, and everyone but me could see it! I wanted a perfect world, I wanted the impossible.

So with occasional giggling teenage highs came the awful deep trough of depression, and it was desperately deep.

About three days before I was due to go back to boarding school one of these despairs hit me. It had great timing, 11 p.m. at night.

I wept and wept trying to hang reasons on any peg I could think of. Most parents would have told you to get a grip on yourself, or would have talked things through with you. Not Mum. She was going to cheer me up. Actually I'd sunk so low I didn't want to be cheered up, there was a cruel satisfaction in being so depressed! But Mum didn't talk about depression, she announced we were going out.

"Where?" I was astounded.

"Anywhere, just out."

"But it's 11 p.m!"

"So!"

So out we did go, we got one of the late buses into town. Everything was shut, it was nearly midnight, the last of the drunks were singing and drifting haphazardly home.

But Mum made me grin, in spite of not wanting to. As we walked along the pavements, orange glow from streetlights shimmering on the wet surface and puddles, Mum made me chuckle, then giggle, then burst into laughter. I can't remember all the daft and funny things she spoke about. I do remember ending up in a swing park where, with no one watching, Mum and I swung on the swings, laughing till my sides ached, and a window in one of the nearby flats shot open and a voice told us to, "Quit making so much noise and clear off!"

We walked home, as the buses were no longer running, and I felt peaceful once more. Okay, I couldn't imagine my schoolfriends' mothers swinging on swings at midnight, but I began to realise that they were the poorer for it, not I. I can remember these times just as I can the times with Dad because they were so unique, so different to the normal rule of things.

I had by now become a fan of The Corries. It would have been hard not to do so, and the music meant a lot to my young mind, and I began to see the fans as more than a sea of faces. They were warm, human people, who loved the music for the same reasons that I did, because it was emotive, encouraging, amusing and a balm to those with other worries.

The Corries did not perform to you, they performed *with* you.

You became part of their family, or clan; you belonged. Fans wrote beautiful letters to Dad and Ronnie, they sent gifts and helped with contacts. On the whole a very nice 'down to earth' group of people, from all walks of life, and all age groups.

I held Ronnie in great awe and respect. Part of this was because of his convincing 'ferocious' act on stage. He was always very quiet off stage, but when I was small I kept thinking he'd give me an awful row if I did anything wrong! And yet he'd tease me and joke, and I remember going to his own childrens' parties and enjoying the fun there. It never dawned on me that Ronnie could ever be shy!

Dad took me to Glasgow one day, to be part of the audience for a BBC half-hour concert. It took all day to film, and I learned an amazing amount about the interaction of the cameras, and what the director had to do. There would be interruptions from the sound crew, and often we would have to clap before a song was even sung. One of the crew would hold up high a rolled up newspaper... the signal for us all to clap like mad, and when he lowered it we were to stop.

Dad and Ronnie were great, going over again and again certain verses, and in between filming keeping up a friendly banter with the crowd. They were always fantastic with their audiences. Dad had the greatest regard for the disabled people, possibly because of his own ill-health, or perhaps because of his treatment by his mother. I remember him talking with enthusiasm and pride about the night of one concert, when they had wheelchair races with some of the disabled fans, up and down the aisles in the audience. It was an evening of great hilarity and friendship, and drew the fans closer to The Corries.

17

With my 'O level' exams now behind me, and having earned Dad's good humour, Sheena and I were taken for a hillwalking/camping holiday. By now Dad drove a Range-Rover, and as we left Edinburgh with Handel's *Messiah* thundering from the stereo loudspeakers, we were very happy, excited and felt that nothing could go wrong. (HAH!)

Near Laggan, Dad drove the RangeRover on to one of General Wade's old roads, the surface of which was littered with boulders. After several 'sea-sick' miles, we came to a level square patch on the left hand side up the incline. A stream rippled and burbled down minute waterfalls on the other side of the road. By now it was beginning to get dark, so we hastily pitched camp, Sheena and I still shrilly talking with 'adventure' excitement. Poor Dad was coping well until a huge herd of nosey cattle started inching up fom the twilight gloom. Sheena and I had suddenly found the place hopping with frogs, and we raced around picking them up and admiring them.

"Karen, Sheena, can you see that old, fallen-down dyke surrounding us, build it up as fast as you can!" Dad urged frantically.

"Ooh, Dad, do we have to?" Sheena whined.

"Look at the frogs, Dad, there's hundreds of them!" I tried to distract him.

"Build the wall NOW, look at the frogs later!" roared Dad, as he furiously hurled great boulders at the wall, and leapt orang-utang-like in front of the cud-chewing beasts. They all paused mid-chew, totally astounded at the uproar in their quiet pastures. At last, exhausted, covered with dirt, but having saved our pitched tent from the ravages of fierce marauding herds, we stopped to admire our stone-walling technique. And, as if in disdain, the last cow ambled off after its friends, — demolishing three foot of dyke in the process!

We slept well that night, but awoke to midge bites, inevitably some of the culprits had managed to sneak into the tent. Eggs and bacon for breakfast cooked by Dad, and tasting great. The waterfall, next to camp, made washing-up easy.

Then it was hill-walking time, and we struggled into our boots, checked our equipment and set off up the stony road. Though not sunny, the morning was bright, and more importantly...dry. After a while Dad led us off the road and up into the hills, following his map and occasionally checking his compass. His long strides ate up the miles, he looked happy, hair blowing everywhere, wearing his favourite scruffy jumper and tattered corduroy trousers. Still keen to impress, I'd try to match my stride to his, (which must have looked stupid, considering I had shorter legs). Poor Sheena, being the smallest, tired the quickest, and we had to make lots of halts for her. Her enthusiasm never waned though, probably like me, she realised this was a precious and valuable time, this holiday with Dad. After many hours 'trekking' we reached the top of Geal Charn, and sat down with our backs against the reassuring roughness of the summit cairn. The vast view stretched before us, dappled in light and colours, hollows and hills. We ate our lunch up there, peaceful and happy.

Dad leaned closer and whispered to both of us,

"Very carefully now, look just behind the cairn, there's a large herd of deer about fifteen feet away from us,"

"What?" said Sheena, not quite catching Dad's words. But I peered round cautiously. There they were, so close you could almost touch them, hundreds and hundreds of them. My eyes feasted on their graceful legs, gentle eyes and cautious manner, as Dad explained to Sheena again.

"WHAT! Where?" she loudly exclaimed, and shot straight to her feet. They all rocketed away with incredible speed, and a soft thunder and rasping of short hooves in heather. Within seconds they were down the slope, across the valley, and pausing only briefly on the summit of the distant hill. I'm not sure who was the most surprised, the deer or Sheena!

We trudged back to camp, weary, but with images of space, wilderness, and endless time, untarnished by man-made objects. The midgies were lethal back at the tents, and I was certain our evening fry-up had extra midgie protein in it! Dad gave us rags soaked in paraffin to tie round our necks, but nothing seemed to deter the little monsters.

Our task the next day was to find Loch Spey. It was the source of the powerful River Spey, and Dad knew it would be leaping with salmon. Not only that, but with the drought the level of the water would be down. Well, we set off in the blazing sunshine, carrying rucksacks, fishing rods and lunch. For miles we trudged like intrepid pioneers, and I was almost getting the hang of Dad's long stride too! Dark and empty

Breakfast tasted great! — Dad and Sheena

stone walls of an old bothy came ever closer with each step taken, and when we peered inside, we discovered piles of deer legs lying on the dusty floor. With morbid fascination, we mused on who might have been responsible for the slaughter, and what had been the fate of the rest of the animals. It was a pleasant escape to step out ino the sunshine again. Not far from the bothy was a huge peat hag or bog, and yet on the hillside was evidence of ancient terracing. Dad's imagination took over again!

"This was once a thriving wee croft with a small family, they lived here with their sheep, and one or two cows," he said.

"And hens?" piped up Sheena, lost in Dad's imagery.

"And hens," agreed Dad, "Then over the years, a bog formed on the side of the hill. It grew bigger and bigger, with each wet spring or bleak winter, till it slowly engulfed the farmer's crops, and oozed its steady advance, down on to the flat land near the bothy."

"Why is it called a peat hag?" I asked.

"Because it's a huge, deep hollow, filled with a wide surface of mud, on which grassy tussocks grow. And you could actually walk right out to the middle of it, without realising your danger. At that point, the whole of the surface would start to shake like a jelly, and suddenly cave in beneath your feet!"

Sheena's eyes were by now almost standing out on stalks, and her lower jaw hung very much agape. I knew it was the silent calm before the storm, and any moment now the "Why?" questions would start in their thousands! Then much to our consternation, Dad started walking across the peat hag, jumping from tussock to tussock, and calling us to follow. Uneasily I stepped from one grassy mound to another. I was sure I could feel the surface quake, but perhaps it was just my imagination, or nerves. Anyway parent orders or not, we refused to go any further, and wailed and wailed for Dad to come back, terrified he'd be swallowed by the hag. Was he testing us? Teasing us or challenging our courage, or perhaps he was just trying to ingrain a lesson in safety? I'll never know, but back he came and we all skirted safely round the bog.

Singing and whistling (and probably scaring every wild creature ten miles away), we wandered round a hillock, and there, glinting in the hot sun lay the loch. It was sadly depleted by the drought, having shrunk to half its normal size, but the fish were jumping all the time, with lazy, heavy splashes, sending ripples everywhere. We had lunch first, and then I showed Sheena how to set up her rod the way Dad had shown me.

"Where's the hooks, Dad?"

"In the bag, in a grey metal box."

I rummaged around.

"I can't find the box, Dad."

"Oh here, give it to me," he said, and catching the bag, searched through it twice. He became somewhat pale with horror as it dawned on him that he had forgotten to pack the hooks! And as if to taunt him the salmon continued to leap higher and higher out of the water. Dad was FURIOUS, in a cool but deadly 'no sense of humour' way, more at himself than at the pair of us rolling around, helpless with the giggles. It certainly didn't help that I took a photo of him, sitting with thunder written on his face. For a while Sheena skipped about trying to find bendy bits of heather, which she assured us would work even better than the missing hooks. In the end we all lay back in the grass, and watched the little puffs of cloud scud across the blue sky, or eagles wheeling in the thermals. Secretly, I was glad we didn't have to slaughter any fish, but would never have admitted that to Dad.

After another midgie-infested night, we awoke to a low-cloud, dreary kind of day. We went up the Corrieyairack Pass, which was quite an exhausting climb. At the top, the wind howled round us with hurricane force, and it became very hard to stand upright in its stormy blast. Yet the views were eyecatching, despite the low clouds. Perhaps for Dad, it was a

...he had forgotten to bring the fish-hooks!

little more disappointing, because he knew what it should look like on a clear day, and kept giving us great descriptions. Ages later we were on the homeward trudge once more, the mist grew ever thicker in about, Sheena and I ran through it, shouting to hear the strange, unnerving, muffled effect of the fog.

Dad bellowed a warning, told us not to run, but to hold hands, and we'd all get safely back to camp. We paused then, to study the map, and with hot and cold waves of fright realised, had Dad not stopped our headlong rush, Sheena and I would have run right over a steep cliff only a few yards further on. We crawled back to camp, glad to snuggle into the warmth of our sleeping bags, and glad, too, that it was raining, for the midgies had fled for a while.

Sunshine filtered through the tent, in a warm, orange glow, the next morning. Sheena said she had a 'sore tummy', so it was decided we wouldn't walk far from camp that day. After breakfast I played with Dad's cross-bow. He said a fan had given it to him, ages ago, but that he'd never used it, and nor would he, on any living thing because unless you were a fantastic shot, you could wound an animal, which would run off and then take days to die a horrible death. All I shot was the old wooden bridge, across the burn, and that was quite good fun, until one bolt became so embedded that we couldn't get it out, and it's probably there still. Dad taught me to stand, legs slightly apart, resting the butt of the cross-bow like a rifle against my shoulder, line my eyes along the sight, take a deep breath, hold it, and fire! I had thought all you had to do was point the thing.

After that we decided to go for a peaceful walk, and explore the course of the stream. Now Dad was complaining of stomach pains too, so we didn't go far or fast. About a mile from camp we found a very dead sheep lying in the burn, which explained the mysterious sore tums, but I was puzzled as to why I had been unaffected, when I too had drunk straight from the burn, with cupped hands. We boiled all water from then on! As we turned to go back, Sheena mentioned that she had lost her cagoule on the previous day's walk, but thought it might be lying on the side of the road just a little way back. Dad said she could go and look for it so long as she didn't go too far, or stray off the road, as the mist was beginning to return again. So Dad and I started making the tea at camp, whilst Sheena trotted off. The mist came up the valley in thick waves and Sheena did not come back.

Suddenly, looming out of the mists, miles from anywhere, appeared a strange woman. She had white hair, wore tweeds, and in each hand carried a clump of bog myrtle.

"I wouldn't camp here, if I were you," she warned.

"And why not!?" snapped Dad, slightly on edge because Sheena had still not returned.

"Well, this is the Lady's Cairn and strange things happen here."

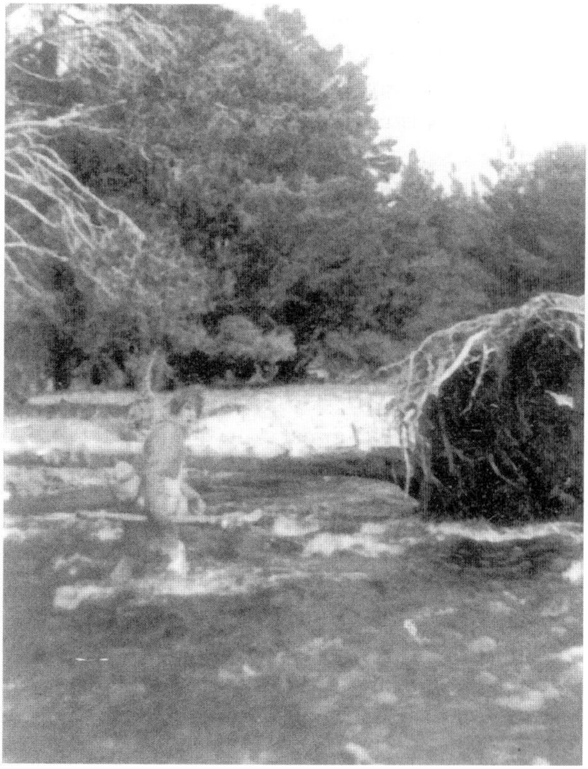

Roy — fishing trip

My wide-awake face betrayed my sudden morbid interest as the strange woman went on speaking. Pointing to a mound of little boulders, near our camp, she said,

"Be sure and put a stone on the Lady's Cairn before you leave, or it could be very unlucky for you."

Then she turned about, and walked straight down into the mist, in the uninhabited valley.

Dad was in a bad humour now, and told me to watch the tea, whilst he went off up the road to find Sheena. Despite his orders, not to leave the road, Sheena had backtracked up the side of the hill, found her cagoule, and was just walking back down when Dad found her.

The story of the ghostly lady was told again and again that

night, as we sat under the starlight sky, watching the red embers of our camp-fire.

Dad was playing the penny whistle and it made a pretty sound in the vastness of that big dark countryside.

As Dad's hauntingly clear tunes played out into the night, I though I heard an echo. He stopped and listened, we all did... It was no echo, but someone whistling in the far distance.

WOW! Did we all get the creeps!!

Of course, it didn't help that Dad had earlier been telling us frightening ghost stories. I could feel the hot and cold sweat prickle on my skin, and my ears became as sharp to sounds, as any wild animal's!

Now and again the whistling would stop, only to start again a bit closer.

Then the shape of a man lumbered into camp. Dad did his 'protective father' bit, and then came back to explain to us. It was only a German tourist, caught by the darkness, and as scared of us as we were of him, that's why he was whistling!

The next morning we drove into Laggan to replenish some supplies, and who should we meet at the local Post office-cum-everything shop, but the strange lady from out of the mist. She was certainly no ghost, and yet another peculiar thing occurred: she had never met Sheena before, and yet she said,

"Ah this must be your youngest daughter. I believe she has an interest in stones and fossils. I have something for her." She went outside to her car and came back with a huge snail-shaped fossil; Sheena was delighted. I was just so glad that the woman hadn't been a ghost after all. Her parting shot to us was again,

"Now do remember to place a stone on the Lady's Cairn, before you leave."

Dad was puzzled, how had this stranger known Sheena was his youngest daughter? How had she known Sheena liked fossils, and how had she known that we hadn't packed up camp yet?

It was midgie 'Hell' again, back at the camp! If you thought you had one in your eye, and put up your hand to get it out, you ended up with the whole hand black with them!

Thousands of them! So we decided to walk to a loch that we could see lying underneath a cliff, very deep, and a mysterious dark green colour. Dad told us it was that colour because of the large amount of copper in it, which was why we immediately christened it the Copper Loch. Although we all set off in high spirits towards it, to my great disappointment, we could not make the last two miles to it. It was so near and so far. Sheena had become exhausted, and was still bothered with an upset tum, so we plodded back to camp again.

By dusk the midgies descended again with determined fury. It was awful. Having mocked at incoming tourists for not being hardy enough to stand up to our native Scottish hazards, we now found ourselves in sympathy with them! Darkness was falling and we'd had enough.

Dad told us we were getting out NOW! We abandoned the tent, and Sheena and I ran to the RangeRover. In the few seconds it took to open a door and climb in, thousands of the bloodsuckers had invaded. Sheen and I, mercilessly squashed them with anything to hand, whilst Dad rescued the most valuable equipment, and threw it in the back of the car.

"Dad, Dad, you have to put a stone on the Lady's Cairn!" I yelled instantly, through a tiny opening in the window.

Dad looked disgruntled but agreed, and wandered down to the cairn — and past it! He bent down and picked up a stone, which he then placed on a different pile of stones.

We had watched all this from the car with puzzlement, then with dawning horror, as the cairn he had walked past, (which we could see as a tall pale column) began to move with him, following him silently, as he placed his stone on the cairn in front. We wound down the windows and screamed and screamed for Dad to come back. He turned, oblivious of the tall ghostly column, which we both were convinced was the dead 'Lady', and strode swiftly back to the car.

We drove even more swiftly from that place to a hotel, which though full, took pity on us.

That was the year the midgies were so bad, they stopped the Inverness to Aberdeen train, and they stampeded herds of cattle, according to all the locals! It helped our wounded Scottish dignity to think that perhaps we were not so soft after all. They also told us that where we had pitched our tent was well known as an old Roman fort site, so no wonder there had been strange goings on there. We retrieved our tent the next day in reassuring, brilliant sunshine,

(Months later, I learnt that the 'Lady' that the weird woman had mentioned, was one in a party escorted over the Corrieyairack Pass in the wild depths of winter. The woman fell ill with her new-born baby in her arms, and with blizzards threatening the rest of the party with hypothermia if they stayed with her, it was agreed to leave her behind. The soldiers promised they'd send someone back for her the next day. When they did come back the woman was dead, but they managed to save the baby. They buried the lady under a cairn, where she had fallen, at our camp site.)

The holiday was drawing to a close, but we still had some more fishing to do. Hiring a pretty, little wooden rowing boat at Laggan, we rowed far out on the loch. Owing to the drought, the water was not too deep in places, but the floor of the loch was very silted up.

After our new education in bogs, I was convinced it was quicksand. Dad patiently taught me how to row, and navigate, which I really enjoyed, but being strong from handling unruly horses, I tended to row too fast, more like a power-boat than a row boat. Dad reduced me to giggles, as he said the fish must be puffed out, trying to catch the fish hooks as they whizzed by! As I left one huge, surging white wake behind us, he impersonated a fish, saying,

"Wow, there go my liver and onions," in a resigned and

mournful fishy voice!

It was understood that if we ran aground, he'd have to get out and push the boat off, as I wasn't getting stuck in any quicksand. We had quite a row when he urged me to take the boat in very close to a sandbar.

"Ooh, we'll get stuck!"

"No, we won't."

"We will, we will! I know we will...and it will be bottomless bogs down there!"

"Just try a bit closer, Karen. Look, you can see the fish!"

Of course, we ran aground right in the middle of the loch, and true to my word, I wasn't getting out to push the boat off. But I did have a problem hiding my mirth, as he took his socks and shoes off, and squelched into all that horrible mud.

It was time to go home. We were sad the holiday was over, and we'd soon be parted again, but we made the most of it, and urged Dad to tell us his funny 'on the road' stories.

One very hot day, he and Ronnie were driving along in the

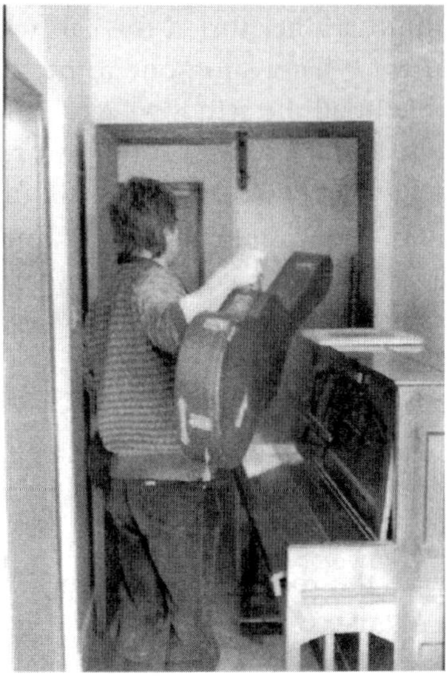

Tour time

"..help!" Roy and Ronnie in Urquhart Castle

Range Rover, on the way to a new gig, having just finished the last one. They were both drinking cans of Coke (— well, that's what Dad told me anyway! —), Ronnie finished his can, and spying an approaching litter-bin area as they were zooming up the road, he hurled the can with all his might, out of the window! What a shot, one to be proud of! There was just one problem, all the windows were shut at the time! The can ricocheted like a bullet, round and round the inside of the car, Roy ducking like mad whilst still driving.

On another occasion Roy and Ronnie were relaxing as they drove up a very quiet country road *en route* to their next gig. Not a car in sight, — when suddenly, a huge wheel shot past them, and rolled and bounced away down the road ahead of them at top speed.

"Some poor bugger's lost his wheel!" said Roy.

Then both he and Ronnie slowly turned to look at one another with dawning fright! It was *their* wheel! Theirs was the only car on the road. Right enough, a few yards further on, the Range-Rover slowed down and began to list to one side!

Later, when we were again on a camping trip, we needed wood for a fire, and we were near a forest track. There on the ground was an old wooden pallet, and one end of it was broken.

"Ah ha," said Dad, spotting it, "Keep the coast clear, Karen."

Then he began lightly to jump up and down on it, bouncing higher and higher, heavier and heavier, as the thing stubbornly refused to break, but became a trampoline instead. He looked so funny leaping up and down with a serious look on his face, his arms swinging for balance like an orang-utang. I wonder what the papers would have said had we been caught!

Sometimes fame could be useful though, and got him out of potential trouble. He was often poaching, and on one loch we were caught by the Ghillie. Dad took off his glasses (he used them for driving), and was recognised as one of The Corries — and was allowed to carry on fishing undisturbed! I suppose it might seem a bit unfair, but then Dad had to make so many sacrifices of privacy for his fame, that it was nice to get some benefits too.

Ronnie and Roy—
rebuilding Urquhart Castle?

18

The Monastery stood hidden, and secret, behind a street of more modern buildings. Dad was like a small child with a new toy, when, after buying it he took me to see it for myself. It was like entering Doctor Who's Tardis! A small shop front in Forth Street disguised the larger building behind. This same shop front was to become the reception area, and secretarial department for Corries Music Ltd. Dad let me through to the back, where a huge and infinitely older set of stone walls reared high and religious, to the old but still functional ceiling. I think the windows were small, but church shaped, and I remember thinking it odd that there was no stained glass to brighten the gloom. The old pews had still been there, according to Dad, but as I looked round at the dirt and dust, hearing the jaunty whistling of the workmen and builders, I felt a little sad about the long forgotten years of neglect the place had suffered.

But Dad was not sad. Enthusiastically, he chatted on about how the place was going to be transformed.

"But isn't that a bit of a shame?"

"What makes you think that?" he seemed puzzled.

"It's just the sense of history the place has, Dad."

"It's quite an important building," he agreed, casting his eyes slowly around the solid determined and dependable walls. "But, rest assured, the framework of the building will be left intact, we'll keep its shape, and as far as possible the windows too." He paused for a moment then added, "Anyway, my hands are tied to a certain extent as it's a listed building, and they have to be preserved."

"So what are you planning to do to it?" As soon as I'd asked that, I realised I shouldn't have!

renovations in the monastery

Dad launched energetically into descriptions, of what room would be fitted where, all the time describing areas and shapes with his arms. He lost me totally, so I nodded as if I understood, and thank goodness he didn't ask me to repeat what he'd just said. After all, it was easier for him...he'd seen the plans. But I did prick up my ears when he mentioned the Rats.

"What rats?" He had my full attention now!

"Oh, there were quite a few of them, and they even had me worried, these are a new race of Super Rats."

"Yugh"...I glanced nervously around. "Are there any here now?"

car boot sale? Ronnie, Roy and Lee Elliot

"I'm not too sure, we haven't seen any for a while, but the amazing thing about these rats...they are at least twice the size of normal rats!"

"Weird!"

"They may have mutated from their original size when they became tolerant of rat poison. It certainly gives you the creeps when they refuse to get out of your way!"

I was glad when finally we exited out through the little shop front, out into the thin winter sunshine.

Our diverse, and hectic lives allowed us little time in the years that followed, to meet often at Forth Street, we were more likely to socialise over a meal at Stirling Road. But I do remember Dad asking me to round up some friends to help with sorting out promotion pamphlets, and record sleeve inserts, or some such thing. It was a tedious boring job, but had to be done, and everyone received a nice cash payment.

When I did pop into Pan Audio (which was another name for C.M.L. or Corries Music Limited at Forth Street) it was nice to chat to the secretaries, or to Forbes Fordyce, Dad's accountant and great friend. Forbes was in many ways one of Dad's right hand men. He often talked about Forbes' wisdom, and held him in great respect, but it wasn't all serious either, the pair had a ready and matching lighthearted wit. Dad was desperately concerned when Forbes was struck down with a life-threatening illness some years later. But Forbes' strength returned, and soon he was 'back at the helm' in charge of all things financial. This was just as well, Dad was as bad as I am when it came to saving. Oh, he knew about good investments, and made quite a few advantageous gains in that department, but he was hopeless at 'taking care of the penny to safeguard the pound'.

In fact, at home, there would be little mountains of coins, thrown haphazardly into old pots or milk bottles, where they seemed to grow, each time he was putting clothes into the washing machine, or the jangling and clanking in his pockets got too much for him. Money really did burn holes in his pockets, and quite often I'd watch with amusement, as he added some more coins to his trouser pocket, and would seem distantly confused as they rolled out through a tattered worn tear, down his trouser leg to clatter in ever decreasing circles onto the wooden floorboards. Thus another 'copper' was added to the growing mountain. These pots of coins, which looked enormous, but must have only added up to about thirty pounds.

But, back to Pan Audio, or CML.

The up-to-date recording gear was often used to record other artists' work, and Roy was very good at encouraging up and coming talented unknowns. He also worked at producing commercials for radio. All of a sudden, my sister and I were whisked off by him to Forth Street one day.

"Where are we going, Dad?" (from Sheena as she leaned over our seats from the back of the car).

Dad cursed as the traffic lights gleefully flashed to red, and he had to brake. Someone tooted a horn impatiently behind him, when the lights signalled 'go'. I was angry, how dare anyone tell off my Dad, didn't they know Dad was always right! "Go on Dad, do the 'V' sign at him, and toot your horn!"

Sheena looked wide eyed with anticipation of some interesting conflict.

"No, Karen," he admonished me quietly, "I don't need to stoop to that, anyway," — he jerked his head back at the other driver's car — "If you've got time to toot, you've got time to scoot!"

My sister and I liked that, and chanted it over and over, and probably made Dad extremely regretful he'd ever mentioned it. (It was again another of his lessons that sank into my life, that illogical shouting and brutish displays of strength will never get you as far as cool debate and sensible reasoning!) As we turned into Forth Street, he answered Sheena's earlier question, which of course she immediately changed to, "Why are we here?"

"I want you to help with some recording we're doing for an advertisement."

Wow! I thought, fame at last. I was going to be in an advertisement, was it for Radio or TV? Self worth, and I dare say vanity, filled me impressively, as we locked the car and marched into the studios.

A number of other people were there, friends, and business acquaintances of Dad, all dressed informally in jeans and comfy jumpers. All thoughts of TV vanished. Dad thanked everyone for coming in at the weekend at such short notice, and then went on to explain what he wanted done. He and one or two other people would wear headphones, from this they could hear the soundtrack for the advertisement. The rest of us on a cue from the headphone people were to clap loudly a set sequence into the mikes. It sounded a bit like a football fans' chant.

Several times we were cued.

Clap, Clap... (then three swift) *clap, clap, clap!*

We did it over and over.

At first I was horrified, then embarrassed...then I took a severe case of the giggles, which nearly set everyone else off. Dad became terse, he frowned.

We kept trying, he became more displeased, it had to be 100% perfect. It was alright for him, he could hear the accompanying music, it made sense to his ears. I kept getting the sequence wrong, nerves were taking over. Dad frowned more and more. He was obviously under some tight deadline. Sheena was much more uninhibited, and being more musical, was enjoying the rhythm of the clapping. I was scared to

Roy on his boat

make a mistake again, so I mimed my claps and Sheena's confident ones made enough noise to cover the loss of mine. Just when I thought Dad's mood had become more thunderous, he suddenly grinned, took off his headphones, and said,

"That's it folks, thanks again for coming in, we'll call it a day now!"

And as we left the studios I realised all that glitters is not gold, and this advertising business could make you feel very self conscious.

I had also seen the total uncompromising character of 'Roy Williamson the boss', in command and under pressure, but unquestionably the undefied 'no nonsense' leader!

The Corries — and fans!

19

Back at home, it was time to prepare for School Highers. The last term at school sped past in a flurry of extra work. Dad and Ronnie were now not just touring the U.K., but Germany, Canada and the States (in 1978), and there was talk of Australia, as well. He even fixed it for me to go and work on a ranch in Arizona, where I could be with my beloved horses; unfortunately the vacancy came up whilst I was sitting my Highers, and so I couldn't go. He always kept in touch by letter though, and it was with great hope that I'd wait at the school notice-board, to see if one would arrive for me! And Oh, when I recognised his handwriting on the envelope...I'd try and read each word of the letter slowly, make them last, but couldn't resist the temptation to rush through all news, humour, and information.

Zetland Place

Dear Karen

At last your photos, sorry for the delay, no excuses except the usual pressure of work, after-tour-lethargy, etc.

I saw a book the other day which I thought might interest you; it's called 'Talking with Horses' so I bought it and will give it to you on saturday (I won't make the Carol Service unfortunately as I've got to go down to West Buccleugh, Ronnie's place.

The book is very interesting, all about "thought communication", sign language, etc. I haven't read it all, just dipping into it here and there.

Well, soon be *Christmas!*

Any ideas, present-wise? an Oxo cube, maybe? or

self caricature by Dad— practising thought communication with horses!

perhaps a drawing-pin or maybe something more useful — like last week's Radio Times — have a think about it.

I left school with a pang of sadness at the ending of a familiar way of life. But I couldn't be sad for long as I had a super summer job, working with trekking-ponies up in Kingussie. I thrived well there, although I felt the family I lived with were a bit uncomfortable with me. They didn't live for horses the way that I did, they probably thought it strange that I didn't go out socialising at night — but once out in the hills with the ponies I was in my element!

Dad came to visit and for my birthday he bought me a moped to help me travel around. It was a lurid yellow colour, and had a helmet to match. Being slightly nervous of it, even after having been instructed in the fine art of moped control, I convinced Dad I wasn't risking my life on that thing, until he'd proved it be safe! So he decided to demonstrate. He looked enormous on this little yellow moped, and to make matters worse, my helmet didn't fit at all, but perched like a huge yellow boil on his head. He revved up the motor, let go of the brakes, and the machine promptly reared on end, nearly depositing him on the flagstones.

With his help I did get the hang of it — eventually! It did brought back memories of the long-ago days, when he used to push me round Lomond Park on my first new bicycle, when I was totally unconvinced that the stabilisers would stop me from falling over.

Sunny summer gave way to the windy whirlwinds of autumn, and I was back once more in Edinburgh. My horse, Pharoah, had been sold whilst I was still at school, but I exercised a pony for some friends. Dad would sometimes come to watch me compete, which made me both nervous and proud, and inevitably I would manage to make a right mess of things! After two years of riding the pony, Dad agreed that I should try to buy her, to train on. However, the owners were too fond of her to let her go, and I'm glad to say that when I last heard about her, she was enjoying a happy retirement with them still.

Along came a new horse, Breeze. He was a cruelty case restored to health by my friend Caroline, and after I came back from Kingussie, I bought him. I took Dad out to see him. The horse was a beauty, jet black, and fine looking. Normally Dad wouldn't get on any horse, his excuse being, "These fingers are not insured," meaning he couldn't perform on stage with broken fingers! To my surprise he did climb up on Breeze on condition that I led him. I was told very strictly not to let go.

So there he sat like John Wayne, and we ambled down to a friend's yard. Realising that his friend was in the yard, Dad hissed down to me,

"Let go, let go!"

I was perplexed, but then I was just beginning to learn about the pride and ego of men! So Dad rode Breeze into the yard, as if he'd ridden all his life. (He had in fact ridden with Ronnie on police horses down the Royal Mile in Edinburgh, for a BBC TV film, so he did have the basic rudiments for keeping control and saving face!)

Dad helped me enrol with the Fulmer School of Equitation, to sit my British Horse Society's Assistant Instructors exam. The course lasted a year as I was working for my lessons and had to earn my training. Once more my days were long, I'd work from 7.30 a.m. to 6 p.m, and then look after my own horse till 9 p.m, get home, snatch some tea, go out with my boyfriend till 1.00 a.m, wake up next morning at 6.00 a.m. to start all over again, six days a week. Sadly, I didn't have a great deal of contact with Dad over the eighteen months, as a result. Occasionally we managed the odd meal out or two, and of course we could talk freely on the phone.

One amusing day, he came to pick me up from the stables, and I asked if he could give my boyfriend a lift as well? Tom was well-educated, well-mannered, good-looking and had a side-splitting sense of humour (and I loved him). How could he fail to impress Dad? But to my horror Dad gave poor Tom the fierce, suspicious, 'No Nonsense' type of grilling that a criminal might endure. I could not believe this man was my Dad, I was appalled and embarassed! Of course, Tom didn't really notice, because he had no idea how nice Dad could be. (It came as quite a surprise to find this paternal and protective side of Dad.)

Most of my boyfriends, over the years, were never invited back to my home. I was too embarassed that they might be shocked, that the contrast between their imagined 'image' of a famous family home-life, and that of the weird, unconventional life we did have, would end any prospects of a good relationship before it even had a start. But most of these fears were ungrounded, it was just my young adult awareness surfacing at the turbulent, teenage time. I was so critical of my own failings and that of my family, that I failed to see the truth of the matter, that every family had its untidy, embarassing or less attractive side, and that it would have been awful if all families conformed to the same ideals. But I was silently self-conscious in those days. Frightened that Mum would laugh or nosily interfere, that Dad would disapprove, or that, 'I might let the Williamsons down'. That was just me.

I did take Tom home a couple of times. Mum told me there was a can of beer in the fridge, and she passed the can to me, and I ferried it over to him. Grinning a thank you, he took it, then with amusement, asked me if I would like to do something about the large knob of butter that was stuck to the side of the it. I was mortified. I should never ever have brought him here. These things did *not* happen in other people's houses!

Mum left the room but was replaced by my teenage sister.

"Sheena, do you want a can of coke? Well, here's some money, nip down to the corner shop, and buy yourself some."

She glanced suspiciously sideways at me, why was I being so nice? But away she sprinted, long pigtails flying, down the two flights of stone stairs. Peace at last, Tom and I chatted, I relaxed, Mum had kept away, sketching in the other room. Distantly, I heard Sheena's feet galloping up the stone stairs two at a time. There was a sudden clank, then a ricocheting clatter, then footsteps thundering back down the stairs again. But I was more engrossed in Tom's stories, so that I scarcely noticed Sheena's laboured breathing, and registered only a flicker of irritation at her as she pulled up a chair and sat down immediately behind Tom and I. Sheena pulled the ring off the coke can: with a 'Whoosh', the contents fountained upwards like a brown foaming geyser, to hit the wall almost to the ceiling and to splatter over me and shower down on Tom. I wanted to die!

Roy — posing as a horse expert!

20

Sheena, at home, was starting to have teenage rebellion problems, this, mixed with unhappiness and insecurity, was more than my mother could handle. I was away working most of the time, and when I did come home, it was to an atmosphere of pending verbal violence. Mum was also unhappy, and she was trying to give up smoking at the same time. She'd often phone Dad, under stress, to complain that Sheena was getting out of hand, or I was fighting with her again. She just couldn't cope. This in turn would bring Dad out to have a 'stern talk' with us.

Life started to become very uncomfortable indeed when I failed my B.H.S.A.I. exam. I had been thrown off a horse, three times in a row, and although the unfortunate animal was from then on banned from further use in exams, it did not help me to know that my more 'cowboy' than 'elegant' position in the saddle, had already failed me the exam in the dressage section. I was bent double with agony when I got home, and that was nothing compared to my mental anguish at having failed.

I was seriously depressed.

Dad was waiting for me.

"How did you get on?" he asked moodily.

"Not so good, I failed," I fought back the tears.

"WHAT DO YOU MEAN! YOU FAILED?" he was furious.

I explained all that had happened. I think he thought I had been abusing my time there, but I most certainly had not. I had absorbed a tremendous amount of training. It just seemed to be my fate never to look the elegant rider!

He started to lecture me. It was all too much. I broke down and sobbed.

"Don't get on at me Dad, it's bad enough for me to bear it. My back's killing me, and I can't even pass an exam in the one subject I love."

"Oh, stop feeling sorry for yourself!" he thundered back.

It seemed cruel at the time, but I know that his refusal to allow anyone to dwell in self-pity, was a survival thing. If you got stuck in the self-pity 'rut', you never got out. Dad taught me, no matter the shock, or loss, kick yourself up the backside, and get on with life. I know he was right, but I do believe an immediate, and shortlasting, degree of self-pity is nature's 'elastoplast', a landing stage before you go on to fight the battle again!

Dad's fierceness that day was the start of a breakdown in our relationship, and although temporary, was to last a couple of years. The tension in the house really started growing between Mum, Sheena, and I. In Mum's case it was a mixture of bitterness with Dad, and the hardship of giving up smoking. With Sheena it was massive insecurity, and with me it was the knowledge that I seemed to be useless at whatever I tried, and that I could never please Dad! The explosive atmosphere was such that I tried to stay out at the horse all the time, and when I did come home I locked myself in my room. This prevented me getting hit by the full blast of Sheena's fury at life as she sought attention, and stopped me being used as a verbal punchbag by Mum. But without my contact, their pressures grew, and grew, with no outlet. Mum was constantly phoning Dad about us, and he was constantly lecturing us.

He decided that I could make a career in art; I wasn't so certain, because all I could draw was horses, but I was pleased to be having in his attention once more. Most days I'd catch the bus from Marchmont, down to Trinity to his house, where he'd teach me to paint in oils.

No matter which house we were in, at whatever period of

time, the art studio, on the whole, remained unchanged! The shape of the room, or height of the walls, may have been different in each case, but still the organised clutter of Dad's painting materials stayed comfortingly the same.

Sometimes there were two tall easels for holding a canvas steady while he worked on it, or to allow a certain painting to dry. The easels were adjustable, and stood like battleweary soldiers, flecked here and there with the colours of escapades with paint on canvas. A smaller easel stacked in the corner was less in use, it was not as rock steady against the power of Dad's brush, and being lower in height did not give a good 'viewing'.

There were unobtrusive tables with haphazard splashes of dried paint crusted on the wood where a brush had rolled off the palette, or Dad in great inspired haste had impatiently knocked paint off his brush, to replace it with another hue.

Battalions of 'hairy-headed' brushes stood side by side in a collection of jam-jars, milk bottles, and occasionally one of his homemade pottery pieces. The brushes he used were varied; long, slender, fine-tipped ones; short, thick-bristled, paint-holding affairs (all with natural bristles). Scattered around, crumpled and smeared with colour were the rags, for cleaning the paint off. Here and there, little exercises in colour contrasts, or sketches on quickly-primed hardboard, could be found — if you searched under everything else! And usually there was at least one hard-backed art-pad with more quick sketches, and occasionally a scribbled verse of a song he'd been working on, or a hand-written timetable of jobs he had to complete that day.

The heavy smell of oil paints pervaded everything, cut through by the sharp scent of turpentine, or the smoke curling in a blue arc from an overflowing ashtray. Roy never believed in finishing a mug of coffee, so there would quite often be three of four half-full ones in various stages of old age! — and the gingersnap biscuits had to be tentatively sampled to find out which half-opened pack was the freshest! It was not that he was slovenly, just that when some great artistic inspiration came upon him suddenly and without warning, all else would be forgotten.

He liked to have the radio on while he painted: I do not believe he listened to it half the time, but its background noise gave him a sense of peace. In fact he often had the radio or tape going when driving, or to listen to last thing at night. It had been one of the things that had been constant throughout his life, since those very young days when he made his first crystal set, I think when he was at Gordonstoun. (He once tried to explain the workings of these crystal sets, but I was totally lost! It was a similar interest which later led him to build a a large and intricate gyroscope.) I think, for Dad, his studio was a timeless place, without demands, where he could to a certain extent escape the pressures outside.

In his own words, from one of his letters written to me when I was still at school:

> ...maybe dawdle down to the studio and lazily dab some paint onto a canvas, put some music on, make myself a nice cup of coffee with ginger snaps and think of you toiling away at Geog and Bilge* (Jealous yet!)

* *Geography and Biology*

Roy's cartoon

At first my painting lessons were fun, and I was eager to please. Dad was trained as an art teacher, but he was against me going to art school because he thought initial style and talent was often drowned in too much 'taught' technique. Yet he himself fiercely began to teach me the mathematics of colour and light, and history of art. He pounded the academics of it into me till I could have yawned with boredom. I painted my horses with the wind in their manes, and freedom in their spirits; they were never a composition of pigments forming light and shadow, they were real...to me. I tried but I couldn't understand why Dad made such heavy weather of it all. Painting horses was fun! He once asked,

"Can you paint nothing but horses?"

To which I replied,

"*You* only paint ships at sea, and I bet you couldn't paint a horse!"

There it was...the Challenge!

By the next time I came for my lesson, he'd painted an Afghanistan rider sitting on a grey horse against a desert background. I had to admit it was good, very good! His knowledge of the horse's form was rudimentary, but his technique in painting carried it off. Dad had learned too, and for a while, he eased his criticism. We had happier days, both working together at our easels in his studio, taking breaks for coffee and gingernut biscuits...(he had a real fetish for those!)

I loved going round art galleries like the Scottish National Gallery and the Royal Scottish Academy, with him. He'd speak in hushed, very serious tones about this painting or that, whilst I tried in vain not to make those awful squeaking noises with my rubber-soled trainers on the grand, highly-polished floors!

He gave me painting exercises to do at home, studies in light and shade. At first I worked very, very hard at them, but Dad was a perfectionist and was very free with criticism, and hardly ever gave praise. A resentment began to grow in me as I began to believe he liked to 'pick on me'. I failed to see the

'The Challenge'— Roy's painting of an Afghan horse

real reason which was that Dad genuinely thought I had talent and was desperate to push me hard to succeed. He admitted years later that he had been wrong to teach me that way, but at that time he drove not only everyone around him in a hard way, but himself more so.

Escaping from pressures at home, I used to spend every moment of the day out with my horse, leaving less time for the seemingly thankless homework that Dad had set me. As a result of this, one exercise — a study in black in white — was dashed off in a mere ten minutes and still slightly wet when I brought it to him! I cringed as he studied it, waiting for the row; but to my amazement, he was very enthusiastic about it! I couldn't understand this at all; it seemed the more I tried the more he criticised, the less I worked at painting the more praise I received. Looking back I now realise that my laboriously-prepared 'homework' exercises must have looked as lifeless and boring as I found them to paint, whereas he spotted signs of talent emerging in the uninhibited spontaneity of my hastily-finished sketches — a case of not seeing the wood for the trees!

Dad was a perfectionist and his own work required 'blood, sweat, and tears' whereas my best work came from quick unshackled, instinctive strokes. I also failed to understand that people can be irritable with you because of other frustrations that are nothing to do with you at all. I loved the good days, with the sun filtering in through the windows, and Dad's stereo system playing beautiful, classical music, as we worked away. When he did drop a word of praise, I wore it like a golden crown all day, happy with everything. His great sense of humour used to make me laugh at the silliest of things. We were much alike: reclusive, happy with our own thoughts and able to keep ourselves occupied without a necessity for other people around us. Yet both of us had the

(left): detail of a seascape by Roy

(below): a bowl made by Roy

ability to keep others entertained, as well as sharing an imperative need to have some time entirely alone in our own 'space'. When we couldn't get that, and pressures began to trap us...*Wow*!...look out!

On one such occasion, I'd been working on a large canvas depicting a girl riding a horse bareback, cantering into a pond in a forest of Silver Birch trees. I had 'blocked' everything in, finished horse and rider, and the water. I was very proud of it so far, I knew it was the best I had ever done. Finally the painting was almost finished and I called Dad over to view it.

"What are those?" he asked sarcastically, pointing at the canvas.

"Trees," I sulkily replied, knowing full well that he knew exactly what they were!

"Karen, have you learned *nothing?* A kid at junior school could do better!" he ranted.

All the bottled-up frustration that had been welling up inside me finally broke loose, and I burst into tears. There was just no pleasing my Dad, once more I had failed. Then I got angry, very angry, I told him exactly how I felt about the painting. He cooled down then and asked,

"Do you have *any* ambitions in life?"

I did not reply.

He asked again.

How could I tell him that my only ambition was to be happy, to own a horse, and have contact with Dad; that I didn't mind what I worked at to achieve it.

"You must have *some* ambitions!!" he thundered.

He had always driven himself, forwards and upwards, striving to be better and better. I knew at that time he couldn't understand the simple things that made me happy, so I replied,

"No."

We had a row then, and I ran home in tears.

But home wasn't a refuge either, only when I was out on the horse, away from people, could I find my inner peace again.

I started 'escaping' to the horse any moment I could. The tensions at home grew worse, and after a fight with Sheena (which, looking back, I know was neither of our faults, but just a blowing-off of the tensions), Dad was notified, and he told me I'd have to leave the house.

Why me? It wasn't my fault! I was hardly at home as it was, and even then, I stayed locked up in my room for most of the time. I contemplated the horrific situation. I would have loved to have turned and walked out and never gone back, but I wasn't my Dad's daughter for nothing, I knew I'd have to live off the streets and worse still part with my beloved horse, Breeze, the only happy aspect in my life at that time. I was furious, and Dad seemed to like tormenting me!

Of course I was wrong to think this, and Dad admitted to me years later he had felt very bad about the whole affair.

But I had a lucky break in finding work with a mountaineering shop owned by 'Graham Tiso'.

They were terrific, a nicer bunch of people you'd be hard

Roy and Ronnie *photo: Bill Robertson*

put to find. Down to earth, funny, friendly, inventive, sympathetic and above all...*normal*. If they only knew the good they did me. Now I had two escapes, the horse and work, to keep me away from the minefield of emotions at home. And when I did eventually return home, I'd lock myself up in my room again. So thankfully I saw even less of my family. When Dad phoned it was always to speak to Sheena now, which suited me fine, as I still felt hurt by him. Gradually Sheena received more and more of his attention, which in the long term did her just as much harm as my estrangement from it. I think Dad had learned from his treatment of me, and now switched to the other extreme with Sheena. When suddenly this blast of benevolence was withdrawn years later, Sheena couldn't cope and became very depressed.

During this time, one happier occasion was Dad's boat, Sheena and I had both watched her whilst under construction, and Dad was tremendously proud of her, having designed her himself, based on the old Zulu-type fishing vessels. It had been fascinating watching her grow, from a skeleton of ribs and frame to the finished product ready to be launched. He named her the *Sheena Margaret* after Sheena

Roy explaining his design for the Sheena Margaret *with a model*

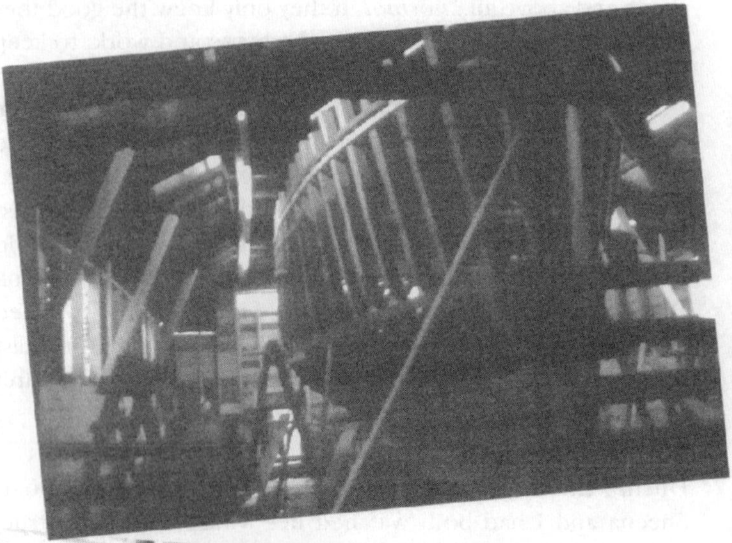

(top): the building of the Sheena Margaret
(left): my sister launching the Sheena Margaret *with Roy looking on*
(opposite page): maiden voyage

who, (having heard Dad complain how much the boat was costing to build), had offered to give up her pocket money to pay for her — 50p per week!

The Corries were very famous now and every performance was packed out, with more and more fans up and coming. So the launching of Roy Williamson's boat in Arbroath created quite a stir. The local press covered it with articles and large photographs; there was a dance at night which went on for ages, (especially when Grandad, the worse for too many pints, commandeered the microphone to give *his* rendition of some well-known Corries songs!)

Dad and I kept fairly clear of each other in the months that followed, I think still hurting from each other. I even thought twice about going to The Corries concert, but hurt as I was, I was still immensely proud of him, and so I went off to be captured by The Corries' timeless magic once more.

21

Then disaster. 27th January 1982.

I had travelled out by bus from work to the stables. It was a dark night, but as was our routine, I put Breeze, my horse, out for a run around in the field behind the stables, whilst I mucked out. My friend put her grey pony out with him.

Unknown to us, some vandals had opened up a section of fencing up near the busy main road. We heard the clatter of panic-stricken hooves on tarmac, and realised that the two horses were out. My heart thumping wildly, I ran after them, — by now they were out of sight. The other girl ran with me, and together we flagged down a car and gave chase. Caught behind a convoy of cars, we could only watch helplessly as the black shape of Breeze hammered along the white lines in the middle of the road, cascading thousands of glowing sparks, from his panicking, sliding, shoes.

Then the sudden glow of oncoming headlights, silhouetted poor Breeze, and suddenly went out. By the time our car drew alongside, there was no sign of my horse. I was out of that car before the wheels stopped turning. The car that had hit my horse was a wreck, you wouldn't have even recognised it as a car. The driver, thank God, was unhurt, saved by the window frame on his side. Others pulled in to help. Someone told me the horse was in the field. Jumping into the field, over a gate, I started sprinting in the darkness; fear, a wild, hot and cold, charge of desperate energy surging through me like a growing tidal wave.

"Breezy, Breezy!" I cried.

I heard a friend (from the same stables) start to scream in a horrible, shocked, high-pitched way. There was no mistaking what that wordless scream meant. I spun round, back towards the smashed car, my legs pounding in rhythm. The girl with me tried to slow me down by holding onto my anorak, but that night I was filled with a mad, insane kind of strength, and I just hauled her behind me. People tried to prevent me seeing, and one man tried to hold me still. But supposing what they had found was not Breeze? Supposing he wasn't dead? The sea of strange faces around me might not know! A torch was thrust into my hand, and I peered over the hedge.

He lay dark and still, neck and shoulder broken, eyes open in surprise at death...seeing nothing any more.

I was taken to a nearby hotel and urged to have a drink, but I had gone totally numb, I had no emotions, no ideas, no nothing. I just couldn't grasp the fact my only secure friend and source of freedom, had just moments before been taken and crushed lifeless...Breezy...*Dead...how could he be*??

A cup of tea was set before me, but I don't think I even drank it or if I did I don't remember. Then the police came to take details, and to urge me to move the carcase. It was against the law for it to lie near the roadside, and had to be moved within twelve hours. My new-found friends helped me out, by saying they would phone the local hunt kennels, and they agreed to take poor Breeze away. Through the anaesthetic of shock, a message rang loud and clear in my mind... 'Phone Dad, Phone Dad,' he'd know what to do, I couldn't seem to handle things any more.

I couldn't get through to Dad, so I phoned Mum to contact him. She got the message wrong and told him the horse *and* I had been hit by the car.

What he must have thought, as he drove speeding through the night... He was realising what I meant to him, and on the opposite side of Edinburgh, in a wee hotel, I was realising what Dad meant to me. The old arguments and hurt seemed so trivial now.

When he arrived, he asked me what had happened, and I tearfully explained, my voice catching with great grief-stricken sobs.

Dad reached out and held my hand.

Not for years, had we had family contact like this, and it gave me a shock. A good thing really, it brought me out of my stupor. Dad took me back to his house that night. On our way past the roadside where poor Breeze lay dead, he slowed the car, and asked if I wanted to go and cut a bit of mane or tail, as a keepsake to remember him by. I couldn't face that, and said, "No."

We drove away.

Dad's girlfriend made us both coffee when we got home. I was still upset, so that when she said, "Don't worry, you'll get another one," I broke down. No one seemed to understand that it was more than just a horse who had died that night. What I had lost was a real friend, and he could never be replaced. Animals are not like cars, or other inanimate objects, there are no two horses the same just as there are no two people exactly the same.

The next day I went home, and the day after that, I went back to work. But it was Hell leaving work to stand at a bus stop that would take me home to my locked room, and not to Breeze.

Over and over, the sequence of events played like a film in

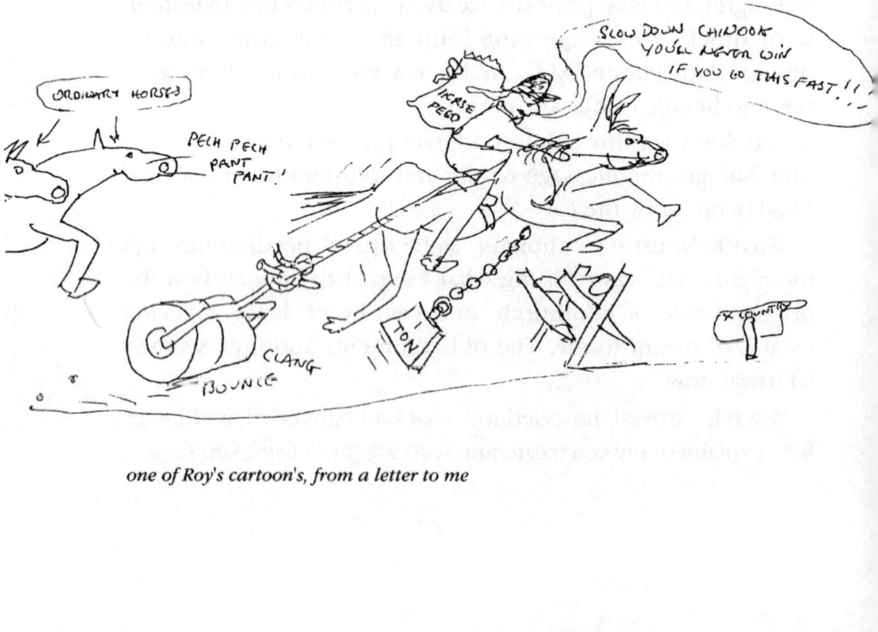

one of Roy's cartoon's, from a letter to me

my mind. I kept re-living the accident, every image so clear, like a film that keeps rewinding and playing all over again.

I was unaware of it at the time, but it was a real turning point both for me and Dad. He came with me to the office where Breeze had been insured, and after two weeks, armed with the insurance money, I sat beside him in the car as we toured round local stables, and dealers' yards to find a new horse.

Mentally I was not ready for a new horse, but desperately I needed to fill the awful, empty, free-time Breeze's absence had left me. Clever Dad came wearing his roughest clothes and his beat-up old pick-up van. We looked at a few horses, then tried a dealer's yard outside Edinburgh.

I tried out several horses, I was still not really following things, moving automatically, and with habit, persuading myself that I was not replacing Breeze, but buying a horse for a friend.

Dad stood sternly in the centre of the arena whilst I cantered round, the owner of the stables talking 'horse' to him, which of course he didn't have the slightest clue about. It was always a set of society that he avoided like the plague. (I think there were shades of his aristocratic mother still haunting him. Yet he sometimes seemed peculiarly drawn to that class structure.)

Oh, how proud I was of my Dad, doing his best, being in a place he'd rather not be; and by doing this, showing he cared at least that much for me!

There was a chestnut mare with a squint ear, black spots, and a habit of sticking her tongue out at people, to scrounge polo mints from them. Chinook was duly bought, and I loved and hated her. I hated the poor mare because she was not Breeze, yet loved her for helping me get over him. (Today I love her as much as Breeze, because she means as much now as he did then.)

22

Life returned to normal again, I was busy with the horse, social life, and work.

And now and again, I'd go for a meal with Dad. It was good to laugh, share stories, and entertain once more. Dad was a master storyteller, and I remember one of his ghost ones.

The Corries were on tour, and one night they stayed at a hotel near Elgin. It was very late, and Dad went to his room. He took some of the more valuable instruments with him in case they were stolen. In particular, his old, antique, wooden flute, with silver taps and rings. It was his pride and joy of the wind instruments, and he kept it locked up in a long metal case. Placing this carefully on the mantelpiece, he then set about getting ready for bed.

Above the bed was a light fitting, with a metal grill around it, and a long string that you could pull, whilst in bed, to put the light off. Dad switched out the light, and settled down on his back to sleep. Just as he was drifting off, there was a loud *'Thwack!!'* and something hit him heavily on the chest. Quickly he pulled the string and flooded the room with light, and found that the grill had fallen from above and was lying on his chest. Setting this to one side, he put the light out, and tried to sleep again.

'Whang!! Clatter!! Bang!!' — the sound loudly sped around the dark room. On went the light again, for Dad to find that his hairbrush, which had been on the dresser on the other side of the room, had been hurled against the opposite wall and ricocheted off it to land on the floor.

photos: Graham Falconer *The Corries*

"Alright, you guys, enough's enough!!" Dad roared, expecting to find a line of cat-gut wire attached to it, leading out of the window directly to Ronnie's, or Lee Elliot's, practical joking fingers! Yet on close inspection there was no trace of any wire. Dad was all for jokes, and vowed to pay them back in the morning! He switched out the light, and lay back.

'*Chuckaa, chuckaa, chuckaa*,' came a soft sound over and over again. Dad was now becoming tired, and determined to sort this out once and for all. He put the light on, and checked the whole room painstakingly over...nothing.

He stood where he was and switched out the light.

'Chuckaa, chuckaa, chuckaa,'

The noise started up again. His ears detected the exact

source of it, and he switched on the light. Once more everything was quiet. And it was no practical joke... He crossed to the mantel-piece: it was the silver taps on his flute being played, whilst still being locked up in its little case!

Call it a gift, call it a curse, both Dad and I had some kind of sixth sense. We could walk into some places and feel fine...others...and there would be horrific, physical feeling of dread, unhappiness, and tragedy. You had an urgent feeling that you had to get out quick.

We had both seen so-called 'Ghosts', or strange phenomena, and so we were quite able to believe others that had too. Sceptics will laugh, but perhaps what we had was an instinct that every animal and child is born with, (but perhaps some people lose as they grow up to rely more and more on fact and reason?)

Our 'Ghosts' may simply have been other telepathic recordings from a long time past. Dad often told me that science was only beginning to learn things, and it was frightening to think on the huge amount that it didn't know.

His father before him had been plagued by poltergeist activity. Dad could remember when he was only eight years old, being woken in the middle of the night by a terrible noise coming from his father's locked study. With his brother he crept to the top of the stairs, his mother, and father cautiously investigating downstairs.

"Get back to bed, Roy and Robert," she scolded, as she caught sight of them, and was now on her guard against violent intruders. The great noises from behind the door in the study ceased, as soon as my grandfather entered. There were papers and books everywhere, scattered all around. Even the locked oak pedestal desk was open. Yet there was no sign of forced entry into the room, it had been heavily secured with shutters on the windows, and only a sparrow could have got in via the chimney. It was never explained.

He bought me a western saddle for my birthday, actually...if truth be told, I requested that he should buy me a western saddle. I was filled with wonderful visions of riding out into the sunset, or lost on the range, and deemed it only viable if I had a western saddle for the horse! I had learned early on that the key word to use when making such outrageous requests was, 'Investment'.

"Won't that be a little expensive, Karen?"

"Oh, no Dad, I'll be able to learn a new method of horsemanship, and the saddle won't lose money, I can always sell it on at a profit in a few years' time!"

He frowned, rubbed a hand thoughtfully across his chin. I could see he was nearly persuaded as I sneakily explained, "Just think what a good investment it will be!"

He looked round at me, the restless debate gone from his face, and replaced by a grin of light spirit at my devious wheedling and manipulation!

photo: Bill Robertson

photo: Graham Falconer

The saddle was a beautiful, second-hand, authentic American one, with handtooled black leather, and a bright yellow saddle pad. The horse looked fantastic in it. So we set off to 'ride the ranges' — or rather, the housing estates of Sighthill! It soon dawned on me that riding English style in a western saddle was not going to work, for one thing every time I jumped a log, the roping horn would knock the wind out of me. I needed to learn more. Failing miserably to find a qualified western teacher within travelling distance at that time, I did the next best thing... I wrote to an American magazine that supplied all the ranches. It basically focused on breaking broncs, and cattle, but to their credit they published my letter. 120 replies winged their way from that far flung country to my home. People from all walks of life, girls and boys, ranchhands, people keeping horses for pets. (I had a suspicious one from a life term prisoner, who said he kept Shetland ponies in the back of his car! This worried Dad a little!) I think he was somewhat amused that I'd had the ingenuity to span countries in search of some education, but I believe that ignorance leaves you unfettered to try 'mad, out-of-the-blue' ideas!

I was pondering over which person to reply to, when the phone rang. It was a guy from Canada. He was very keen to see me learn 'the right way of western horsemanship,' and didn't mind phoning. He'd had horses all his life and quite a few stories about them. Realising that I would learn far better with a two-way immediate conversation, I agreed.

At first everything was okay, the guy was great, told me about the different kind of western saddles and training. Dad was keen on hearing how I was doing too. But as the year went by, my 'pen-friend' started phoning me up at five or six in the morning. I was always polite to him, but it was wearing me down, not to mention my mother, who was always woken by the piercing loud ring of the phone. Things were snowballing rapidly away from my original request. The guy was embarrassingly generous too, sending huge bouquets of flowers, or expensive leather belts, or duckdown jackets for me to wear when riding. The phone calls became more and more frequent, and I was embarrassed that I could not send equally expensive gifts: as it was, I couldn't even afford to phone Canada myself.

Then one day my long-distance friend announced he would be coming over to visit me. How awful, I thought with great horror, he'll see just how poor we are compared to him! Dad, however, thought it was a fine idea...

"It's always good to have contacts," he advised me.

But I still felt nervous about the whole thing.

My Canadian pen-friend, or should I say 'phone-friend', was to stay at Dad's as there was more than enough room for visitors at his house. I was given money to go and buy a new dress, Dad didn't think my holed and tattered jeans would make a good impression. He also reminded me to have some beer cans in the fridge.

Doomsday had almost arrived, and I had worked out all the places my visitor would like to go and see — most of them connected with horses of course! I waited for him to phone from the airport to tell me when he would arrive. But no call ever came. Nobody was more annoyed — and glad — than I! I felt a bit embarrassed because of all the hard work Dad had gone to, in encouraging me, but I also felt relief that my pen-friend was still just a distant phone-friend.. As he did not get back in touch I thought the matter was closed. Hah! I thought wrong!

Dad, with his endless supply of friends and contacts, had unearthed one in the same town as my vanishing phone-friend. This contact was a retired detective, and he tracked down my phone-friend very quickly, and came back with his new telephone number to Dad. I was mortified. Dad suggested I phone my friend.

I did this.

And the deep Canadian drawl on the other end apologised, but said he'd been mugged outside a bar and all his money stolen, so he hadn't been able to fly to Scotland. I would have believed him, if only he'd phoned to tell me. The phone-friend is now gone, but what remains is my memory of Dad's power of communication in countries, thousands of miles away, and that he often went to great lengths to 'fix' things for his daughters, he was happy if we were happy.

There were still tensions between Mum, Sheena, and me at home. I was lucky, and managed to escape most of it by just not being around, but Sheena's problems became so great, that communication between us was lost. Dad startled us all one day by announcing that our house was to be sold, and that he was going to buy each of us a small flat instead. It was to be part of our inheritance so he told us, and, 'Better you should enjoy it when I am alive, than when I am dead!'

But I saw right through that rather morbid statement, to me it was another sign that Dad really did care about us; after all, he could have by law wiped his hands of Mum and I. She was divorced and I was over eighteen. Mum was rather annoyed about us all splitting up. This I couldn't understand as she had been so annoyed about the tensions and arguments when we were together.

Flat-hunting with Dad was great fun, we looked at quite a few, and always Dad taught me: how to look for dry rot, damp, woodworm, faulty wiring, and whether the building was perhaps under a compulsory purchase order for a road going through! Wow! were my eyes opened. At last a super little flat was found. Nothing luxurious, but cosy, and near the centre of Edinburgh.

Our two cats, that had been with us since eight years beforehand, moved in with me. At first it was real camping! No cooker, fridge, nor bath. Dad asked his girlfriend to help decorate as I had no experience with that kind of artistic bent! Before the wall was papered up again he drew a huge ship on the bare wall. It was comforting to know it was there, like a child's night light. I cooked on Dad's camping stove, and did most of my washing by hand, or at the launderette just across the road. But it was definitely home. I'll always remember the thrill of unlocking the front door for the first time. The slight twinge of, 'can I manage?' swamped by the huge thrill of freedom and peace. For my birthday, Dad bought me a little black and white TV all of my own... I could hardly believe it.

Sheena stayed in a Guest House, until she was found a nice flat in Tollcross, and Mum was bought one in Leith, again not far from the centre of town. We'd meet up for a meal, and it was like a breath of fresh air, all the arguments were gone. And going to Dad's for a meal became a regular occurrence for Sheena and I, on separate occasions, and we were becoming closer to him now...it seemed he'd dropped a lot of the hostile guards with which he'd fronted the world, and now enjoyed our adult conversations; ours tinged with youth, his with wisdom.

I had mentioned to Dad that now I had a flat of my own, I'd very much like a dog. He seemed to view this as a disaster plan! But I went ahead and bought a cheeky Jack Russell pup, from a friend. I think Dad was quite aghast, until I told him I had named the pup 'Corrie' after him. He was quite chuffed at that, and later became very amused by the little dog's antics.

The years passed with a fierce swiftness. I had hardly time to catch my breath. I gave Dad and his girlfriend a lot of space, and I think that's why I got on so well with them.

Independence was mine now, with my flat, horse, work, and friends, but something was missing, something niggled away at the memories locked deep in my subconscious. Week after week, I'd spend my hard earned cash on...potted plants. Armfuls of them, and they'd fill the living room. Of course they'd all die on me, so off I went to buy some more. Then I really went 'off my trolley'...and bought two budgies! Now the cats had to stay in the living room, the pup in the hall, and the budgies in the bedroom...in case they all ate one another, one day. Looking back on such madness, I realise now that I had a subconscious hunger for the green fields, forests, and farms. Probably, the years at Stobo had impressed me more than I had realised then.

Roy and friends, on the Sheena Margaret *at Muirtown Marina, Inverness*

2 3

Dad told me he was moving up north to Morayshire. It was sad to see him go, but the biggest heartbreak was when our old house at Trinity was put on the market to be sold. The wealth of memories in that house echoed down the years. The 'ghosts' of Sheena and I, giggling as children, and the parties, and impromptu concerts. Yes, it hurt to see it go.

For a number of years Dad lived in Forres, Morayshire, where he bought a huge old Victorian house. I had never gone up there to visit him, because there was no-one to look after my horse and other animals, and after what had happened to Breeze, I became a little worried the same would occur to Chinook whilst I was gone. But we kept in touch via the phone and letters, and he kept a rented flat in Edinburgh, as a base for tour-time.

After a couple of years writing to him in Morayshire, I felt very guilty that I had never gone up to see him. I could hear the disappointment in Dad's voice, every time I said, 'No I can't', so I found a trustworthy friend to look after Chinook, and nervously I trundled north.

The train took me through the huge, snow-capped mountains, down to dazzling lochs, and finally into the fertile area around Forres. The sun shone, the flowers bloomed, total strangers beamed at me and said, 'Fit like, quine, morning!' There was a lack of hustle and bustle, hardly any bad temper to be heard. The local paper had half its front page devoted to the story about, *'The telephone box has been vandalised'*. (In other words, they must have had hardly any vandalism, for such a thing to make such large headlines! It wouldn't have even been mentioned in Edinburgh!)

I was met at the station and driven to Dad's house. It was

house was three stories high, and shaped like a shallow T. It had a well-tended garden, and the house was immaculate inside, not a dust speck anywhere, and just as well, because Dad was very allergic to house-mites. For all its comfort, I found the house terribly depressing. I had that weird feeling at my back, when I went from room to room, and it seemed the house was in a state of endless depressed waiting. But perhaps I was just picking up loneliness when Dad was away on tour, or was it people from years before?

Strange things happened in that house, you could hear doors opening and slamming shut upstairs in rooms that had no-one in them, and most commonly in the room above the kitchen, I heard taps being turned on and off in that room; and one day the radio switched itself on suddenly, full blast and almost mockingly, and then turned itself off again. Over the years there was a runaway electric bill, even though the house had its wiring checked, bills questioned, and a new meter installed; nobody ever got to the root of the problem.

I was surprised that he wasn't aware of the strange feeling, but he was so tired when he came back from tour, that all he wanted to do was relax in front of the log fire. He built a lovely wall round the garden which trapped the sun, and gave privacy. We often sat out in that, discussing politics, inventions, and where the world was headed. On turning the old stables into a recording/painting studio, Dad removed a flagstone just outside, and underneath it he discovered the leg bones of a foal, laid out in the shape of a cross. It seemed a bit creepy, and hinted of dark shades of the secret society bound by the 'Horsemens Wurd'.

Dad, like me, loved his own space and privacy, and would lock himself in his studio for hours, painting away at his easel, or working on a new piece of music.

In the sitting-room small boxes of all shapes, colours, and designs, could be found adorning the shelves of golden pine. Dad was fascinated by their craftsmanship. Having acquired the skill of creating, not just music, or paintings, but marvellous furniture as well, he was no doubt attracted by the genius of other craftsmen's work.

There were mother-of-pearl inlaid on ebony, rectangular boxes, and other little but heavy, brass boxes, with rough etchings drawn onto their sides. He loved the very small and simple wooden boxes, the way they so sweetly opened, or closed, and the joins so discreetly hidden that you would think the box had not so much been made as evolved as a whole. Here and there throughout the house Turkish rugs, with their natural dyes, gave a mellow, ancient feel to the rooms.

The mystery of the Middle East also drew him, and quite a few expensive and heavy books on the subject stood on the sitting-room bookshelves. Contrasting vividly against the ancient past was his great curiosity about the great unknown, the future, and especially space exploration. Fact and fiction sat shoulder to shoulder. And then there were the old books, hardbacked, out-of-print, editions covering bothy ballads, and long-forgotten ceilidhs. Some of his books on boats and sailing were also of a fair age, but much loved, and wonderfully

two bones — Roy's dog, Jock,

and...Roy!

descriptive of the old square-rigged vessels, tall ships, or diagrammatic of the wooden-hulled fishing boats.

He painted many sea-scapes. I thought them excellent, but he was always self-critical. On the walls you could find a couple of drawings or paintings by his daughters, and certainly some other artists' work that had intrigued him in a gallery, but his own splendid stormy seas, and valiant square-riggers, were either still in his art studio, or sitting haphazardly in a corner of the sitting-room, where now and again he would remember to look at it, criticise it, and take it away to work on further, or give it away to any friend that noticed it. And yet his own paintings were better than any he bought out of the galleries, in my opinion.

It was only during the last eleven or twelve years of his life

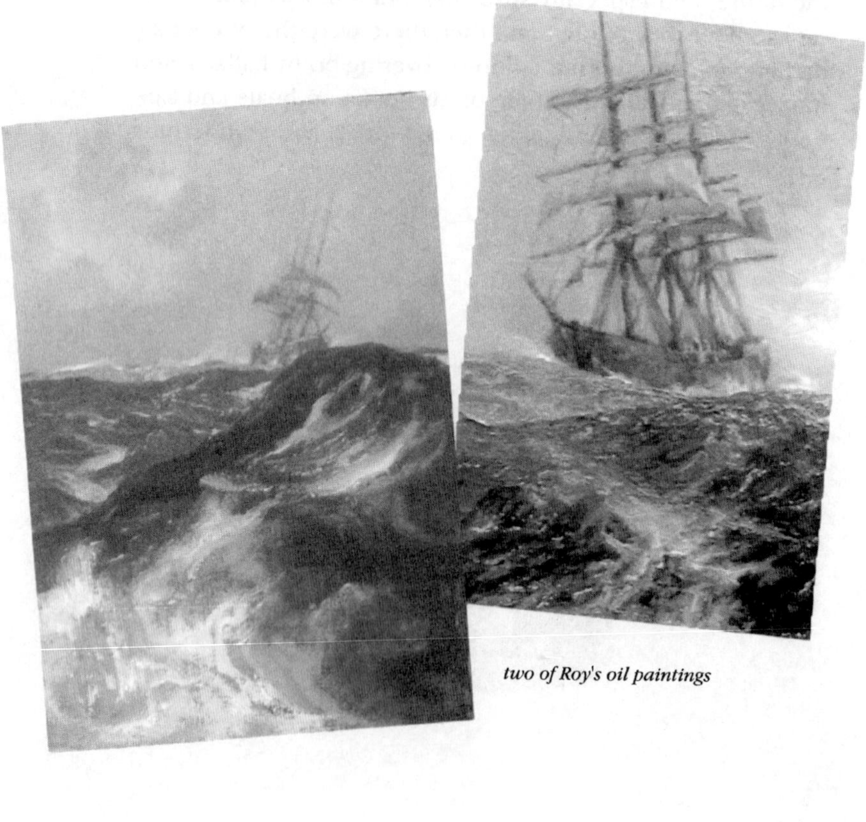

two of Roy's oil paintings

that he began to give his work its rightful place in good frames on the walls. But I think this was because it was his ambition to one day hold an exhibition of his paintings; and ever the perfectionist he could openly be extra critical, and corrective, viewing them in his mind's eye, the way he thought the 'critics' in the galleries might view them.

There was a deep love of all things old, and this reflected in the tasteful choice of antique furniture that was displayed in a discreet but purposeful way. Probably, too, the fascination for the good strong use of materials, and the warm, mellow, seasoned wood, triggered his interest. Or perhaps there were memories, of his distant, and not often mentioned, childhood, subconsciously trapped in furniture designs from those other years! But I digress...back to my three day holiday.

We had fun, lots of it. Dad drove us all round the local countryside. Little narrow roads, with no white lines or traffic signals, in fact hardly a passing car! Wild flowers sparkled vibrantly, amongst the long grasses on the verges, and two-hundred year old trees, of every species, canopied overhead in green cathedral arches. Everything was clean and clear, and wild birds and animals flitted here and there, gleaming and glossy. At Randolph's Leap, the thundering water fell frothy and white over the rocks. Up at Califer Hill the view stretched forever into the far distant, hazy horizon, and down at Findhorn Bay the molten sun sank into the everchanging, many coloured waves, from out of which dolphins leaped and played.

Off Hopeman Harbour, the seas were rough, and cascaded forcefully over the harbour wall. You had to shout to be heard above the fury of the wind. Later we drove through Gordonstoun School grounds, and Dad made me laugh with his tales of his schooldays there and at Hopeman.

Then just as suddenly my three days were over, and I was back on the train heading home.

To my surprise, I had enjoyed my holiday, but more than that, I had found somewhere, thanks to Dad, equal to my childhood paradise of Stobo. Relieved to find my horse still in one piece when I got home, I quickly settled back to work. Images of green places and silver waterfalls haunting my thoughts. I wrote to Dad and when I could afford it, gave him a ring on the phone. Soon another weekend was planned.

It turned out to be even more wonderful than the one before, and as I sat in the train, homeward bound for Edinburgh once more, I decided I'd very much like to live in such countryside. I don't think Dad took me seriously at first, and it was not until my next visit sometime later that he realised I meant it. The train going back to Edinburgh that time was slow and melancholy, and reflected my feelings. Tears welled in my eyes as I left the beautiful countryside behind and headed for the pollution of the city.

There was a real force inside me urging me to move, and I obtained an old copy of the Yellow Pages, and wrote to every shop in Forres asking if they would employ me. But really it was a wasted effort as Forres preferred to employ people living already in the locality. Catch 22!! I had to get a job, to move up north, and I had to be living up there to get a job!

Dad came to the rescue once more, saying that for six months only, I could live at his house whilst looking for employment. The whole thing seemed chancy, but I accepted.

My father couldn't tolerate cat hairs, because of his asthma, and I had no funds to kennel the cats somewhere for six months, nor would that have been fair on them. I tried to find homes for them, but to no avail: I just couldn't face having them put down, the cats had been with me through all my troubles. In tears and heartbreak, I finally said 'Goodbye' to them at the Cat Protection League in Edinburgh. It was not a happy day.

Then came the farewell to the people I worked with, people who had become dear friends, and also some of my relatives. At last, dog, horse, furniture and equipment were all loaded onto a friend's horsebox, and we set off for Morayshire.

Inevitably, visiting for an odd weekend had been one thing, but staying all the time was less easy: I resorted to my old plan of spending all day away with my horse, and looking for employment. I lasted all of two months living there.

So Dad decided to use my flat in Edinburgh as a base whilst he was on tour, and in exchange bought a cottage up here for me to use. We had searched and searched, and I was getting desperate. We found one old ruin up on a hill. It had three walls, and half a roof, and I said to Dad, "I'll take it, I'll take it!" so keen was I to move.

Dad smiled at my daftness, and took me to see more properties over the next few weeks. Some were in the town, but still not very suitable. Then one day I found an advertisement for a little rural cottage with some land with it. The people selling were asking far more than I could expect Dad to part with, but the place was so ideal. We obtained the keys and had a look round. Never before had a place felt more like home. It was very old and looked a little dodgy in places, but it had a friendly and comforting feel to it. It reminded me of Granny and her flowery apron and freshly-made scones. It felt a part of me.

Dad poked and prodded around the cottage, made terrible 'Oh No!!' noises of disgust at nothing, for the benefit of the girl from the estate agents who was listening. And we all trooped back pessimistically to the car.

As soon as we were home, we were all excited! It was 'touch and go' for many weeks as negotiations went ahead to try to lower the asking price. At last transactions were completed, and I moved in with two friends. Dad told me, later, that he fully expected me to come back to Forres six days later, as it was December and winter had set in — true, the cottage was damp, all three of us got bronchitis (the place was damp not having been lived in for six months), but no way was I going back to his house. I was *home!*

My horse moved into the old woodshed and life happily burbled on. I quickly obtained work, showing tourists round a nearby castle. A fantastic job, and only ten minutes cycle ride away.

It was fun meeting so many happy people and making lots of new friends. (Dad was quite impressed that I was employed in such historic surroundings!)

About every second weekend, I'd cycle to Forres, to see him, and grab a cup of coffee. I'd inherited some of Dad's story-telling ability, and amuse him with my anecdotes of the horse, work or the days I helped a friend on her farm. Occasionally he would come out to see me at the cottage, I was delighted, and oddly, a little shy! I had a sneaking suspicion that he liked to come out into the solitude and quiet, to sit at the porch in the sunshine, with a mug of coffee in one hand, and a cigarette in the other, and take a deep sigh of relaxation. No traffic-sounds, just the quiet wilderness around around the cottage.

Soft guitar-notes played into the evening air, as he practised on my guitar, the one he'd bought for me so many years ago. I think he loved my cottage too. In many ways, he may have wished he could trade his fame and hectic lifestyle for some of the tranquillity of mine. We still had the odd game of chess, and he still beat me easily! If anything was being thrown out of the house that they didn't want, he would sometimes bring it out for me. I'd always be excited to see him. As excited as when I waited for him all those years, to take me to riding lessons. There was a harmony between us now. I think that his aversion to the childlike Karen was in the past, as he discovered he could talk 'adult to adult'. We became very close, as father and daughter. We talked about favourite subjects, and he even spent time enthusiastically stroking the horse, and talking about her funny ways.

Birthdays and Christmases were hectic at his house, with special meals prepared. We all ate till it hurt! and then stories were told, or we watched videos.

To keep fit, Dad was encouraged to go cycling and jogging.

But more and more, when not on tour, he seemed to just want to lie back in front of the log fire and watch TV, or to paint in his studio.

At first we thought he was just enjoying himself, but gradually it seemed that his energy levels were falling in a worrying way, and he started taking lots of vitamin pills, and herbal tonics; he went to have private tests for food allergies. Dad, and his best friend Davy, had spent a lot of time working with his boat, the *Sheena Margaret*, but the berthing of her, the upkeep and maintenance, plus tax, and a charter deal falling through, now made her continued upkeep impossible. So poor Dad advertised her for sale. I equated how he must have felt with how it would feel to have to sell my beloved old mare. He was resigned to it, though, and he did feel a certain relief when she was finally sold, and the burden lifted off his shoulders.

"After all, Karen, I designed her. It is I who created her; that won't change."

24

The tests on the food allergies came back positive, and there was quite a lot that Roy now had to give up.

That alone must have cost him withdrawal stress, but also, before every tour, for two to four weeks at least, he would 'come off the asthma spray'.

He would become absolutely reclusive. Even those closest to him were not allowed to stay with him: he wouldn't go out, moved as little as possible, and suffered horrific asthma attacks, for which he denied himself the use of an inhaler. By cleaning out his own system of the Ventolin inhaler, he concluded that he would boost his own natural immune system, to fight the attacks, and then he should require only a fraction of the Ventolin when he want back on tour. Dad had always been slightly hypochondriac about germs, virus, and infectious illness, but I think it was an instinctive response to the very real illness that he'd endured as a child; as if he was preparing himself for an attack before it came.

His standard of living rose too; gone was the beloved, battered pick-up into semi-retirement. A brand-new, posh, silver Volvo was parked in front of the house. I felt that it was new and unfeeling, lacking the wealth of memories wrapped up inside the rusting old van.

Dad was often impressed by other people of high standing from all walks of life. He was very concerned that he should appear bright and intellectual himself. He was all of that anyway, but I feel he was always striving for some unobtainable goal.

But the old familiar Dad would still reappear, nice, humorous, happy, helpful, and relaxed. For all his interest in a seemingly high-class social world, he was right there for the underdog, and helping the needy, when it counted. And was always 'Dad' for us.

I remember clearly our walks in Grant Park, Forres, at night, no one else around, just Dad and I, under a silver-studded, star-lit sky, putting the world to rights, or spotting shooting-stars and satellites, our two dogs, Jock and Corrie jogging on ahead. Dad was always keen on the night sky!

One evening, when I was alone in my cottage at about eleven o'clock, I decided to check that all was well with the horse for the night, and that she hadn't gone down with colic. Tiptoeing outside, I discovered that the whole sky was lit up with Northern Lights. Above the cottage was a huge black 'hole' ringed with a circle of silver, and then, like the spokes of an umbrella, great wide beams of light arched down to the earth all around me. Up and down, shimmering and pulsing, ran electric flickers, and over in one corner was a turquoise and dark-red patch, strange against the deep night sky. It was something a 'Spielberg' film would have been proud of - and I half expected some heavenly choir to

"Good morning!"

start singing. Instead I rushed indoors, to phone Dad, and they went out to watch the overwhelming display too.

Autumn was a special time of year in Morayshire. I more than ever felt that I belonged to the area. After all...Mum had been born in Nairnshire, Granny had come from the Black Isle, just across the Firth, Grandad had worked the great gentle Clydesdales on the farms around me, and of course Dad's childhood roots were here too. The trees formed everchanging mantles of green, brown, copper, gold, red and yellow, and threw their leaves to the wind in shimmering, colourful confetti. It was the time of year when wood-smoke hung aromatic and misty, round the rooftops of the town, and the great 'V's of migrating geese honked their way across the skies, sometimes against the backdrop of the huge, yellow, harvest moon. One evening, Dad brought me some logs for the fire, which was a kind thought of his (although it probably seemed less so to the person who'd laboriously stacked them in his woodshed!) and whilst he stayed for coffee, he seemed tired, and for the first time I noticed a haggard wear and tear in his face. He began to talk about retiring from The

Roy at home, with Sheena

Corries. I agreed that he should,

"Far better to be like me, Dad, not a penny to spare, but a happy way of life!"

Already The Corries had reduced their tours, and now made just enough to live comfortably. But even so, the endless driving, eating fast 'junk' food, and staying at different hotels, were having an exhausting effect.

I had by now managed to reclaim one of my cats from the Cat Protection League in Edinburgh, which was fantastic, as I had almost given them up for lost knowing that the C.P.L. rehome as many as possible. Kitty loved the freedom offered her and soon settled in. It was a good time for all of us...

...But it did not last long.

Dad ran me home from Forres one day, and because I had my bike, he took the old pick-up van. I think he was glad to be back behind the wheel of it again, but a tenseness rose within him when he asked me to unload the bike from the back, saying that he couldn't manage it. He was embarrassed and angry at playing the weak male. All his life he'd been proud of his strength and fitness. It was obvious that the strength was disappearing, and he was frustrated by this.

"Don't worry Dad, I don't mind! After all, what are kids for!" I joked.

He smiled back.

On another occasion, he'd come out to screw a tie-up ring for the horse into the wall for me. He was again unusually tense and snappy. I tried to work out how I had upset him, but then realised it wasn't really me who he was angry with. A job that would have normally taken him three minutes to complete, took him half an hour, his hands shook so much, and the strength was gone from his arms.

'Too much Ventolin inhaler,' I told myself, knowing as a fellow asthmatic that an overdose gave me the shakes.

Dad and I went in to have a game of chess. It took longer for him to beat me, and he asked if I wanted another game?

"Maybe next time, Dad," I replied light-heartedly, "You

exhausted me!"

Mostly he liked to just sit and smoke, quiet and relaxed, with the countryside stretched all around. Now and again he'd tell me stories.

"Did I ever tell you about my pet Jackdaw?"

"No, Dad," I lied.

"Well, all the kids at school had pets, and some were wild birds. We used to train them to fly up onto the roof of the school at the beginning of the day, and at the end of the day, the kids would hold out their arms, call the birds, and down they'd swoop in seconds. And it so happened, mine had asthma!"

"A Jackdaw with asthma, Dad?" I said in sarcasm.

He grinned, took a long puff on his cigarette, and continued, "Yes, and mine used to crawl up a wire to the roof, wheezing like mad all the way. By the time school was over, the bird had only just gained the roof, and gave a look of resignation, and began to inch and wheeze his way back down again!"

I laughed and laughed, not so much at the story, but at the way he *told* it. Dad had a rare gift for making the words come alive.

He started to become much more unwell. I'm not sure if the fans noticed it, that night at the Eden Court concert, but I was aware the fun and lilt of the show was gone. Dad played with all the talent he'd always had, but with a soul set on enduring rather than *enjoying* this performance. Back at home, he began to have dizzy spells, headaches, and feel totally shattered. Sometimes he'd stumble into things, or want to spend more and more time asleep during the day. At first the local doctors suspected a middle-ear infection, affecting his balance, and he went to hospital for tests for this, but on leaving the doctor's room, he collapsed. It soon became frighteningly apparent that this was not just a middle-ear infection, nor a virus.

About that time another much-loved member of my family,

my horse, was at Death's door, and had to have specialist attention at a horse hospital in Edinburgh. The night after night ongoing depression, and the fear that I might have to play God and order for her to be put down, was draining me of my spirit.

But I had to keep jovial for poor Dad, who was now going through a very frightening time, and needed strength from all of us. The new Corries tour was cancelled as Dad went into hospital for more tests.

It was late one evening, I had been sitting in front of the log-fire practising my guitar, when the phone rang. It was Dad.

"Bad news, love," he softly spoke, and my soul fell deep off a precipice as the words... "***BRAIN TUMOUR***" branded like molten metal into my memory.

His voice talked on and on, and I tried to be strong for him, I fought as hard as I could not to break down, but the gasping sobs tore from me, and I could hear his voice start to break in return. But my Dad had a willpower that was immensely tough, and he turned the situation to humour

Roy — on the beach and in the hills

again. He'd always had that knack.

"Don't worry, Karen. It's amazing what medicine can do these days. People are having brain tumours removed with no problems at all...

"I've to have more tests to see what kind of tumour it is, that's all. Who knows, maybe I'll get a new brain! Your old Dad's not 'throwing in the towel' yet."

There was an increase in the journeys Dad had to take to and from hospital, some of which were at night. During these uneasy times I took over looking after his house, and dog, Jock. Relatives phoned me most nights, very depressed, and I tried to give them hope and courage. Thus we swung, on an exhausting see-saw of optimism, pessimism, and back to optimism again. Sometimes it seemed never-ending.

During this time my well-loved cat was hit by a car, and managed to crawl back to the cottage to die. There had been an upsurge in speeding traffic and joy-riders, and it was not the first time that animals had come off worse. Because of worries about Dad, the horse, and now my cat, a change grew in me. I became very, very angry. I actually took to marching up and down my road, with a huge pitchfork, gleefully looking for cars speeding at 100 mph.

(Thank God, they all kept clear on that occasion!) I eventually cooled down, and announced my 'war' on speeding traffic to a local newspaper, only this time, my threat had changed from pitchforks, to summoning the police. Dad was impressed about all this, and chuckled with humour about me battling the world with a pitchfork! He recalled previous incidences of my waywardness, when I'd nearly (by accident!) run over the Duke of Edinburgh when my horse bolted. People had teased Dad endlessly about how it was bad enough ousting the Queen's National Anthem with *Flower of Scotland*, without resorting to physical violence! Funnily enough, Dad was proud that I'd written to the local papers about the cars (in the same way he used to be pleased when I managed to have the 'Williamson' name printed in the results page, after a win showjumping).

Each weekend I'd cycle round to see Dad when he was at home. He still enjoyed his privacy, and once a week was all, initially, that the family thought he was up to. Even then I sometimes found that he'd gone to bed too exhausted to stay awake.

He was a night owl, always had been. He'd sleep in until early afternoon, and work his best from two am until five am in the morning; I suppose a life of working on stage at night must have established his 'body clock' into that cycle.

At this point, as far as I can remember, he still worked fairly hard on his paintings, and was developing a new sound in music, over which he was very excited. He called it his 'Whale Music'. The deep love of these sea animals inspiring his musical talent, through the veil of his headaches and dizzy spells. I did notice that the colours in his paintings became more grey and subtle, compared to the lively colours he had used in earlier years, but at the time just put it down to a change in Dad's style, not his illness. I never let on just how dreadfully depressed I was by his ill health. But night after night, I'd cry myself to sleep, and be haunted by dark mindless dreams. I know that I was not the only one either! The horrible thing about it was that we had to keep it absolutely secret. The media would have dived like vultures for a story such as this.

Always a private man, Dad needed more than ever his privacy. The good times were beautiful, a sad wonderful beauty, and we grew far closer than ever before. Often, we'd sit around the kitchen table in his house, discussing this problem, or that, or perhaps telling each other funny stories. Dad seemed so warm, so unharrassed. I suppose in a way he was, all the problems in life were trivial now, compared to this one *ugly* problem, that reared like a solid brick wall above us all. Sheena came up to visit too, and Dad seemed increasingly keen to have his daughters around.

Dad phoned me from Edinburgh, one night.

"Hi, love."

"Hi, Dad, how's it going?"

"Okay," And with his thoughts for the future he made me feel that it was important to him that he had my approval of his plans to marry again. He then went on to talk about the operation, and finally finished with some nice words to me, to which I replied...

"Well, Dad, you are a Dad in a million."

A few days later, a wonderful letter arrived from him...not the usual humour and joke, but a baring of the heart, which in turn touched mine. I wrote one of equal feeling and love back.

Dear Karen, Hi!

I'm sitting here listening to music and letting my mind wander about a bit, quite relaxing really! And thought I'd just pick up pen and paper and drop you a note (a rather rare occurance I'm afraid).

I am, and always have been, absolutely hopeless at communication, perhaps that frustrated part of me is what comes out in my music, who knows.

When you arrived on this beautiful mud ball we call earth and chose me as your Dad you should have spotted the little label across my brow — 'Damaged Goods'.

I'm being light-hearted about it but there is an element of truth there.

Well, Karen, you said on the phone something about a 'Dad in a million'. I'd just like you to know that I consider you a 'Daughter in a million', too.

In some of my darkest moments I have often gained strength from relecting on your courage and honesty, yes, and your stubbornness too.

When I have been really down and wallowing overlong in self-indulgent moans, I *have* asked what would Karen's advice here be. And the answer would come, "Get up off your butt and do something!" or words to that effect.

It has angered, confused and frustrated me that I have known you experience grief, on a scale that I

photo: Bill Robertson *Ronnie (left) and Roy on stage with the combolins*

have been spared, and I have found myself so inadequate in coping with that.

It comes as something of a shock to realise that in many ways, looking back on things, I have learned more from my children (Sheena has her strengths too) than ever I taught them!

...It is an old adage that one has to earn the right to be proud of someone. Sometimes I feel that I have not earned that right, but whether I have or not, I am proud of you. And grateful too, just for your existing.

Lest all this should be too serious (and, dare I say it, emotional,) let me just say your sense of humour too has played its part. Often on a long boring journey in the van on tour I've found myself smiling at the memory of one of your stories and the way you live them in the telling!

(I sneakily like to think that whatever gene governs the 'funny bone', you got from me!)

So there we are don't worry. I'm not going soft in my old age, I'll still be your rather stiff and distant Dad, but underneath it all there is something that I don't have the words for.

By the way, these are just my jottings; it's not a letter that requires a reply.

love from Dad x x x

The tests results came back...

The tumour was highly malignant.

He had to be operated on right away.

He was frightened about the operation, but immensely courageous too. Writing his Will couldn't have been easy for him.

The doctors had been frank. There was risk. The tumour was huge, it had probably been growing there for years. He might wake up after the operation paralysed, a vegetable, or not wake up at all. The thought of waking up unable to paint, play the guitar, or sing, tormented him far worse than death.

I again stayed up north, to look after the animals, Dad's house, and dog, but was on standby to drop everything and get to Edinburgh swiftly. Sheena stayed with Dad in the hospital, and I was phoned each night, with an update.

The operation lasted hours, that felt more like years.

I had posted down to Dad a huge white shell, that I had found washed up on the beach and carried back home in my pocket. I packed it in a parcel, with a nice note, telling him it was a lucky shell, and a bit of his beloved Moray coast so that he wouldn't feel homesick. He apparently kept it with him until he was wheeled in for surgery.

Faith and spiritual healers had also been contacted, and Dad felt stronger because of this: perhaps for real, perhaps not, but he was certainly boosted by them. His belief in science, the unknown and unproved, giving him hope.

Of his surgeon he said, "I trust these guys, they've worked with the worst kind of head injuries, and they are the best."

His anaesthetist was more than just a doctor, he was a close friend of Dad's. He could not have been in better hands.

"It was a success," the long-awaited phone call told me,

going on to explain in detail.

I hardly heard the words. I was ***so*** elated. Let them check for any possibility of tiny tendrils left...it meant nothing... My Dad was cured and going to come home!! The operation had been at the worst 90% successful.

A few days later, Dad phoned me himself, and this time I was crying with relief! He sounded weak, a bit slow perhaps, but the hope and happiness were loud in his words. Apparently he'd memorised a song before the operation, and was able to play it just afterwards, thus passing his own test. Poor Dad hated hospitals, and this enforced restraint irritated him, although he was endlessly grateful to the staff there.

On the funnier side, he was starving...for fast-food! And the family had to smuggle in endless supplies of junk food; and I think he even managed a Chinese take-away once, because Dad had gone right off hospital meals. Within days he was becoming fractious and anxious to get out.

The doctors were so impressed that he was allowed to escape days later, on strict orders that he report back for tests.

Then All Hell broke loose, as the news that had been suppressed leaked out. Newspapers were determined to track Dad down, and even managed to find me, up in the hidden depths of Morayshire. Ronnie, and my uncle, Robert, were great at handling that side of things. Robert had always been Dad's distant elder brother, and I had been infected with Dad's awe and respect of him, but now I began to see the gentle, and well-educated quiet man that he was, and to be very glad indeed that he was helping us out.

It was obviously important that the loyal and much worried fans be told something. So one paper was elected, and the good news relayed to the public. Dad had written two letters for my sister and myself, in the event of the operation not being successful. They were words of love, and of his hope for each of us, but Sheena and I never saw them. They were burned as soon as Dad was up and about, a kind of celebration at having cheated death. I didn't mind...words were nothing to the thrill of Dad coming home.

At last, when he was fit to travel, the Volvo took them homewards to Morayshire, stopping en route for a coffee at my cottage. I had prepared myself to expect Dad to look a bit battle-scarred, but even so, it was a bit of a shock! He had two enormous black eyes, his skin was of an ill, pale, haggard hue, and he had a horrific scar and hollow in the side of his head, where surgery had been performed. They had shaved a lot of his hair off, from that side of his head, and this bothered him a little. But he came walking in for a coffee, just like the years before, and whilst I was making it I heard him reach for my guitar and pick away at a tricky, classical piece. I smiled as I handed out the mugs of steaming coffee. Actually, I felt a bit self-conscious, because I had been grinning like an idiot since he arrived. It was awful: no matter what was said...I beamed from ear to ear, and when I tried to talk it must have looked odd, because I had to mouth words through a huge brick wall of gleaming teeth.

Roy and Jocky

They say laughter is akin to crying, but right then my relief at seeing Dad again was making a total fool of me. I think he knew. I know he understood.

"Thanks, love," he said as he took the offered mug, drank a mouthful, and setting it down, began to play on the guitar again.

"Wow! The one thing I was terrified of losing was knowing how to play the guitar!"

"What does it feel like now?" I asked.

"Oh cracking, man, just cracking, like having little brains on the ends of your fingertips!"

"What do you mean?" I was puzzled.

"Well, it's so much quicker getting a signal to my fingers, it's almost as though they can think for themselves. It's great!"

I nodded, and then said, "I see a huge difference in you, a real improvement."

"In what way?" he asked eagerly.

"Well..." I thought for a moment, trying to put into words the subtle difference in my Dad, "You're so much quicker to understand the spoken sentence and reply to it; before you seemed to take a wee while to analyse it."

He was delighted with that observation, and kept bringing it up during the conversation.

It dawned on me then, that though Dad had improved, especially his automatic responses, there was a deep, unnerving change. He had become almost childlike, one minute agreeing to anything, the next being more suspicious. I shut my uneasiness away to the back of my mind, and chatted on. Then after a while, Dad began to feel tired, so they sped off to Forres... Home at last!

25

Over the next few months, it became obvious to us that Dad had changed. He was in many ways taking on a 'little boy' role, and those close to him adopting the 'mother' one to suit. But now and again, like a flash, suddenly the old 'Dad' would smile back at you, and crack a joke, or try to solve a puzzle.

The doctors came to visit him nearly every week, and although Dad was good with them at first, he eventually became highly suspicious of them. Nauseated and ill from the radiotherapy treatments, and all the drugs he had to use, he began to rebel. He'd always been fiercely proud of his physique, and now the steroids and cortizone-type drugs were making him overweight and moody. The Faith-healing was continued, and the use of hundreds of little bottles of aromatherapy, and Bach flower remedies. I contacted suppliers of videos on cancer treatment, and kept an eye out for any magazines, or news items on televison about the recovery of those cases.

At night I lay in my bed and willed my strength over to Dad.

Gradually Dad began to have trouble walking, he couldn't manage the stairs, so mattresses were brought down to the living room, and that's where he slept. Several times he semi-collapsed. Close relatives bombarded the doctors for truth, and were shocked when they heard it.

The tumour was growing again.

And with a vengeance. To make matters worse, Dad had become almost phobic about the drugs, and only pretended to take them. His headaches became quite violent, and he spent nearly all day sleeping in a darkened room.

Some of the family, distraught, phoned me night after

night, desperately needing to talk. I took some to see another of my friends, Sarah Jane. Sarah had been operated on twice recently for brain tumours, and was recovering. Sarah was practical and comforting and gave us hope...for a while.

Then one day the doctor told us, Dad was dying.

I felt the anaesthetic of shock land over me like some thick suffocating fog. I couldn't totally comprehend the words.

Perhaps we had over-rated the doctors remarks, perhaps the doctors were just telling us the worst, so that we would be prepared...just in case. I questioned the doctor and hoped that I'd heard wrong. Again the undebatable words.

"Yes, he is dying."

I went blank. I think I finished the conversation, and then went for a long, sob-racked walk in the woods. I suppose it's nature's way, the shutdown of the feeling and practical side of your mind, so that you automatically shunt around, doing things you can't remember doing.

Or perhaps it was just the enormity of it all. Dad, my childhood god, the immortal 'always-there' person...dying? To be taken away? Not possible. I didn't want to talk about it. Even now, it's a struggle to fish through the web of fog-like memory to tell you what happened.

The hardest, hardest thing I ever had to do, was cycle in as usual to town, and visit Dad as cheerfully as I did in the past. As though I didn't know. Panic would thump my heart, and rasp my breath, as I entered the kitchen. Ill as he was, he valiantly tried to see me in the kitchen, rather than lying flat on his back in bed. His thought-processes were becoming slower, and he was more fussy about his food. No longer any interest in painting, and he couldn't bear to play the guitar. (Probably it was hurtfully frustrating, not to have the quick reflexes that he used to, and each mistake he made on the strings now depressed him terribly.)

But we had good moments too, round that kitchen table, soft moments, unspoken, and sure.

His mind could be startlingly bright, and he always made me giggle at some point or another.

He was moved very much by the thousands of well-wishes from fans, and far-off family, and I think he was most thrilled and excited by the rendition of *Flower of Scotland* at the triumphant 1990 rugby Scottish Grand Slam, at Murrayfield. He talked about that for months. So many thousands singing, with a fierce, patriotic pride, *his* song. His life spent in endeavouring to always prove himself, found a kind of solace there. Never had he been so proud of his fans either. Dad had found a kind of peace in this tragedy, he was surrounded by family that loved him, and a world that on the whole acclaimed him, and yet he still had the safety of his private retreat.

I found out later from the doctors that Dad knew he was dying. He had said to them, I m not going to walk away from this one, am I?

They were frank in reply. But Dad sought to protect all of us from this knowledge. It was almost farcical. *He* knew he was dying, but didn t know that *we* knew! We knew he was dying, but didn t initially know that *he* knew. It called for endless pussyfooting around the subject. Occasionally Dad would test us by saying, When I get over this...

Sometimes I d tell him a funny story about something that went wrong up at the farm where I was helping. He d laugh just like old times, but his eyes would fill with water. I felt the sorrow then, but for his sake tried not to show it. I knew he was steeling himself, to losing us all. It seemed so unfair, someone so gifted, and young, to be under such a death sentence.

Why? Just when we were really getting to know each other. *Why, oh, why??*

The days passed, his speech slowed down more, and he became totally invalid. The doctors put him on morphine to help with the pain, but it wasn t 100% effective, and he kept trying to reduce the dose himself. I wrote to Gordonstoun, his much-loved old school, and asked them for any videos of the school that Dad could watch. The headmaster wrote a sympathetic letter, and one of the masters wives hand delivered two videos to me. Dad played one of them, over and

Roy and his second wife, Nicky

over, telling us stories about his days there. But soon his eyesight began to fail. The family nursed him tirelessly, and with one or two close friends, stepped in to 'babysit', or do the shopping.

My friends at work were very understanding, and gave me indefinite leave. My uncle Robert came up to visit quite often now. He was very sad and yet brave too, and he helped hold us all together. Some generous fans had given us a baby alarm, so that Dad could still have his privacy, yet call if he wanted anything. We'd sit and talk amongst ourselves at the kitchen table, with the rhythm of Dad's sleeping breath in our hearing. Occasionally he'd mumble something in his sleep, and we'd rush to see if he wanted anything.

I remember those days with dread, it's difficult for me to open the forced-shut doors of memory, to relate to you. It was a bad time, only now and again tinged with good moments.

I bought him wee gifts, things that he used to love to eat, cashew nuts, and for his health a slice of real honeycomb. But nothing tempted him. And by now the doctors were coming every day.

Friends of Dad's came over from Holland to help look after the house, and us all. They were truly terrific. Mr Van Hurck drove us everywhere that we needed to go, and cheered us up with stories of his past, or of Dad. His wife didn't speak much english, but what a gentle person and a superb cook she was, and just being close and motherly was a real comfort.

At that point, I still went in every day to see Dad, but slept fitfully at night at home. My cottage is very old, but next to my bedroom is a new extension, built on what would have been part of the garden at one time. One night, I was lying in my bed unable to sleep, the light was on, but there was no point in reading as my mind kept whirling over Dad and all the *'if only's'* with which I could torture myself. Dad and I shared a sort of sixth sense, a kind of sensitivity about certain places. Normally when I felt the gentle pressure, or pushing of signals, I was too frightened and would block it out by reciting a rhyme, or the times table (at which I had always been hopeless!)

But my whole mind that night was on Dad, and my defences were down. That's probably why I saw the ghost. Over by the door to the new extension, two almost transparent colours appeared, like misty clouds of yellow and purple. They moved without shape, round and round, without going out of the corner. It was about 2.30 a.m., and my eyes were well and truly open!

"What the Hell is that!"

The colours merged, and suddenly became the shape of an old man. He was so clear, about five foot four inches, retirement age, not fat, but muscled from a life of hard work. On his head he wore a tweed flat-cap, and his hair was grey. He had a roundish face, and was smiling. Although looking in my direction, I'm not sure if he could actually see me or not. He wore a heavy moleskin type of shirt, of an off-white colour. It was well worn, and the sleeves were rolled up to the elbows. It had no collar as such, just little buttons fastened up to the neck. There were heavy leather braces, holding up heavy-duty cavalry-twill trousers, and he appeared to be leaning on a spade or a stick. From the knees down he was invisible. All this happened in a few seconds, but the most amazing thing was the fact that the man was standing in brilliant, dazzling sunlight, at 2.30 a.m. inside my cottage!

Perhaps a time-slip, perhaps a memory picked up, like an old video tape of a long time past.

I only knew that I was startled.

"No, no! go away!" I cried.

Instantly the thing vanished, back into the yellow and purple misty clouds, but I could 'feel' he was still there. For five whole, heart-thumping minutes, after the clouds had gone, I knew I was not alone! I got up and padded off to the loo, and when I came back there was only me in the room.

Over the next few nights, I had a couple of strange dreams about Dad.

The first one...

Dad and I, up on a huge wall, like The Great Wall of China. It was night, and on each side below us stretched a city. The buildings were very Eastern, but then Dad favoured Persia, and Turkish places.

He was trying to persuade me, why things had to be the way they were, why he had to die.

I was furious, and yelling reasons at him as to why he *did not* have to die! Far from being angry, he patiently explained away all my arguments. I remember running out of reasons to convince him otherwise, but instead of feeling despair, I felt only sadness, and peaceful acceptance.

I woke up.

Was it my conscience coming to grips with Dad's loss? Or was it Dad, in his telepathic way, trying to give me *his* acceptance! Who knows?

The second dream was much more disturbing...

I was standing facing Dad, who was in a wheelchair. He was paralysed, couldn't speak or see, and had horrific headaches. Again I tried to tell him why he must fight it, he must live on.

Suddenly, I found myself in his place, I was in the wheelchair. I couldn't move, I couldn't tell people my thoughts, I couldn't see to paint, the music in my head taunted me because I couldn't play it on the guitar. And the agony of blinding headaches was more than I could bear. I woke up weeping. Even in sleep, I couldn't escape the nightmare of Dad's cancer.

Dad was put on Dia-morphine, and it gave him some relief from pain; it also gave him fantastic dreams, and one or two bad 'trips'. It was fed to him intravenously on a small time-switch machine, but he would, from time to time rip the needle out of his shoulder. At one point he became immensely strong, and rose up, blindly crashing about. Being delirious on the medication, he was insistent on his illusions being real, and it was all we could do to restrain him, and prevent him hurting himself. There were good points too, sometimes he'd dream he was floating past stars, and planets, and he'd be very serene, at other times he'd seem wide awake, and be convinced he was in Barney's Dublin flat. He'd conduct conversations, and have a 'whale of a time'!

Humpty!

When his mind was clear he'd be in his 'little boy' mode, and would ask which hotel they were in now. It would be explained that he was in his own house. "All mine?" he'd exclaim in wonderment and joy, "It's really all mine?"

Roy with Davie Sinton and the fishing boat's gear

2 6

I moved into his house to help look after him; family and friends were doing most of the work. We all handled the situation differently. Some of us would become aggressive to anyone in reach, needing desperately to hurl the helpless rage that was felt at anyone, to have someone to blame, to blow like a volcano for a while and then to be able to cope again.

Sheena went around statue-like, smoking like a chimney, switching from being intellectual and in control, to, on rare occasions, exploding with fury, slamming doors and seeking solace in some empty room.

Being sensitive anyway, I was struggling to cope with the change in Dad, and I couldn't handle the tensions of others as well. I became a text book case of depression, unthinking, unreacting, just being there. It was horrendously difficult to think, my brain felt like cotton wool. When not actually doing something to help, I'd sit staring for most of the time at nothing, almost not breathing, or blinking. I was not at all constructive in my thinking, everything seemed to function only in automatic!

Sitting quietly with Dad was not easy. I wanted to weep, but had to stay strong for him. We talked slowly, about everyday things. For him it was not easy; he couldn't speak much at all, and what could he talk about...the future? Present experiences? His hopes? I tended to rattle on, telling him what everyone was doing, but finding it impossible to tell him how much I loved him. He was hardly eating a thing now, and if he did express a desire for hot water, tea, coffee, or a couple of spoons of scrambled eggs, we all fell over each other rushing to get it. The tension amongst us all in the house grew and grew, the weaker Dad became. Sometimes when I'd sit with him, he'd ask for a cigarette. I always dreaded that, because not being a smoker, I was terrified of how to set one up, and how to hold it in his mouth, and what time to allow him to take a 'drag'.

On his last 'active' day, he told me, "I'm bloody sorry about this, Karen, but it just won't do, I'm going to sort it out! You can give me a row if you want to." He flung back the covers, and tried to lurch out of bed. Even in his weakened state, he still had strength. I called for the others, and he was persuaded him to lie down again. But he struggled to get through some imaginary door, on his left, in the corner, where a large black pot that he had made many years ago stood on a shelf.

The doctors and the district nurse came every day now, and there was one anxious moment when the telephone lines went dead. Frantically I cycled off on my bike to find a coin-box.

It was vital that we had communication with the doctors' surgery at all times now. British Telecom, to their credit, had a man round to fix the lines in a matter of hours.

Dad slept fitfully, and we tiptoed around the house, grating on each other's nerves, if by accident we let a door slam, or a cup fall. The doctors kept ominously warning us that, 'it won't be long now'. But they had been saying that for months and still Dad had managed to hang on in there. I'd lost all concept of time. Dad was fading too swiftly, and yet we all seemed to be in a state of limbo. Robert, in tears, tried to be practical, and after the doctors' advice, he broached the subject of the funeral with us. It made me want to laugh and cry. *My Dad wasn't dead yet!* But still, I knew, Robert was right. When the end came, would any of us be able to handle arrangements? I was useless, just agreeing to everything, without really knowing what was being said. And always, Dad's breath rasping away on the baby-alarm, as we talked. *It was horrible, so horrible.*

He had a panicking dream about me, when one of the family was sitting with him, something to do with me having an accident on my horse. I talked to him, reassuring him I was fine. He called out, Shine, Shine, which we took to mean Sheen, Sheen, his shortened version of Sheena, and she, too, told him she was alright. I couldn t handle some of the others need to blow off tension, and to give us all a bit of space, I ran away...out for a walk on my horse. I needed to think outside of the house, but left word of a nearby telephone number, so they could get in touch with me, and Sheena promised to phone if I was needed. It helped get things in perspective, feeling the fresh air blowing round my head, and the rhythmic plodding of the horse through the woods beneath me. My mind slowly began to whirr back into action. I was only gone a couple of hours, at most, but it definitely enabled me to be a better help when I got back.

Another ghastly incident was when we were told to go and buy our funeral clothes. It was practical, of course. Things were rushing to a head now, but I felt sick with a sense of betrayal, a sort of giving up on Dad by doing it. It had to be done, but I felt so guilty and sad. Worse still, Dad at that point called out, and demanded to know who all the folk in black clothes were, that stood at the end of his bed. At first we said there was no one there, and neither there was, but Dad remained certain that strangers wearing black were in his room. Was he hallucinating, or picking up on our telepathic trauma? It seemed horribly ironic, that he should be so close to the truth.

I had prayed, willed, bargained, threatened, and prayed and willed all over again, to let Dad live long enough to see his birthday, and this he had somehow found the strength to do. And then I was praying for one more day, then another. In a way, it was mental torture, you tried to find superstitious bargains, or gambled on expecting one thing, so that fate would do the opposite! We were all a little crazy at that time.

I knew that I must not leave Dad s side now. Thank goodness, for I now had a wonderful moment with him. I sat with him for a good while, the clock ticking away loudly in the hush of the room.

photo: Bill Robertson

Every so often the 'whirr' of the Dia-morphine machine, announced its administration of the latest dose.

He was quiet now...very weak.

He gestured for some water.

I held the straw to his lips.

He lay back and said, "That's fantastic, love."

I smiled and spoke softly.

He wanted a cigarette.

I lit it and held it to his lips.

He took a long inhale, held it, and slowly released it, "Oh, that's cracking, that's fantastic," he sighed.

We were silent a long while.

I held his hand.

Then I whispered so that the baby-alarm wouldn't pick it up, "You're not to worry about anything, Dad. The Van Hurcks are here, and looking after everything, they are feeding us all so well that soon we'll be enormous," I tried to joke. Then more seriously, I added, "Dad, don't worry about anything, *we love you...always*, and if times get tough, think of Christmas, Dad, think of Christmas."

He lay quiet.

One of the others came through to take a turn at sitting with him. But Dad tried to hang onto my hand, he gave it a reassuring squeeze as I got up to leave.

Robert had a good conversation with him, talking about times past, and Sheena and me. Robert told me later that Dad had said of me, "Yes, Karen's turned out alright!" It was good to know, to have merited his approval, I suppose, that had been my unobtainable goal all of my life, in the same way that Dad had had his.

August 12th 1990...

As we all took turns sitting with him, he became more and more comatose. I was one of those with him when he died.

His breathing had become more shallow, and spasmodic. I gestured over to press the button on his Dia-morphine machine, to give him more pain relief. He breathed more easily for a while. But finally it became obvious that this was a fast, downwards slide.

Even at the end, Dad had one joke up his sleeve. His breathing stopped, and did not start.

And great panicking, loud, gusty, uncontrollable sobs, burst from me...when to our surprise, and relief...Dad started breathing again!

Fighting to the end, as always.

Then he softly breathed, in a sort of surprised voice, and just after that...he moved no more, forever.

The others were practical, although obviously upset, and I was mad at myself for being able to do nothing, but stand there staring at Dad, crying and crying, with mindless abandon.

Then suddenly, though it all, for five seconds, came the most beautiful thing. In the corner, it seemed a door had opened — where there was no door! Through it, I could see a tarmac road, going up a slight incline. There were no white lines on the road, and it was very narrow, on each side was a flat grass verge, and just greyness beyond. But I could see Dad walking up the little road, his back towards me. He wore his scruffy corduroy trousers, and his old black and grey Norwegian-style jacket. In his hand he carried a guitar case, a black one. He stopped, halfway up the road, turned round and saw me. His hair was dark and shining, his face ten years younger, and smiling, he silently raised his arm, and gave a slow, big, wave, then turned and walked on, and was gone...

Alright, the mind can play tricks, and all of us, at that highly emotive moment, were entitled to have hallucinations, I suppose. But I then told the others what I had seen, and I described Dad's guitar case (one I had never seen before) and it was that confirmed he once did have one like it. Also, 'the doorway' of this vision had appeared in the corner where Dad had consistently (in his rambling state) tried to get through the wall. I don't really mind what folk think: I felt a great sense of peace, and freedom, for Dad. It did not, however, stop me grieving, selfishly, for my loss of him, and I had to fight to be strong.

Placing a hand on his still warm forehead, I remembered some weeks ago, when he had risen weakly from the chair in the kitchen on his way back to bed, he had paused behind me, and for a long number of seconds, rested his hand on my shoulder silently communicating with touch and thought. It was so powerful and emotive that I can still feel the strength of it now.

I sat down in front of the phone and contacted every one that should know.

"Hi, it's Karen here, I can't speak much, just to tell you, Dad died, just after three this afternoon, can you tell the others that need to know. Bye."

Mum was the most difficult person to tell. It was her birthday, August 12th. In tears, she said, "Poor Roy," and "What a birthday present," and "Don't cry Karen, you mustn't get too upset," but then she'd break down again.

Thankfully, Ronnie was handling the press side of things, and was subdued but capable on the phone.

After everyone had been contacted, the doctor arrived to confirm Dad's death. He helped us get in gear, regarding contacting the people for Dad's funeral. Numbed with shock, I remember little now, just glimpses of events as though through holes in a cloud. Sometimes you felt like laughing, as if you'd never stop, but the urge ran alongside weeping, and anger, and you tried to keep it all firmly bottled up. I remained quiet, as we discussed the horrendous decision as to which type of wood to choose for Dad's casket. The whole thing seemed unreal and slightly farcical.

We chose oak.

Dad loved trees, and he was so proud of obtaining the last good piece of Scottish oak, for the *Sheena Margaret*. After the undertakers had finished laying Dad out, in the casket, we went in to see him. He was wearing his most well-loved clothes, scruffy corduroys, shoes, and jumper and scarf. We placed his favourite mandolin in his arms. Sheena placed

some of the smooth Scottish pebbles, that he loved, alongside him, so that part of his country would go with him. I cut a long strand of my hair, and laid that between his fingers so that he wouldn't be alone.

The undertakers had neatened Dad up. They'd done an excellent job, but between their work, and Death's, my Dad was not there. The body looked different. The man was small. Dad had been enormous, as tall as a steeple, as strong as Atlas, and his character filled the room when he walked in. This was a doll, a poor imitation waxwork.

I felt again the smarting pang of loss.

People began to come round, to say goodbye to Dad. It was very private, but already the news was out, via Ronnie down in Edinburgh as planned, but also through the local towns, as soon as the funeral hearse had brought the casket to the house.

From being a house of silence, we now played Dad's 'Whale Music' (*The Long Journey South*, the last piece of new music that he had been working on), in his room. It was loud, powerful and yet a shadow of my missing Dad. There were candles lit all around him, and Sheena placed fresh flowers about, flowers from his garden.

Old habits die hard, and nerves, raw and strung-out, we still cringed if someone let a door slam. And there are no words to describe sitting down to tea, knowing Dad couldn't have his.

I couldn't bear it when they came to take him away, the next day. Sheena put more flowers from the garden around his casket, and everyone went to the door to see him off. Everyone, except me. I hid. I didn't want to know Dad had left for good.

Cowardly really.

But I was running on instinct.

I went home. It was better at home. The cottage comforted me. Dad was still there, in the history of it. The tie-up ring for the horses in the stable evidence of his help. My guitar played for me, but also him, and the hundreds of other little things he'd given me, or talked to me about, his humour still twinkling in their existence.

Davy, my father's friend, paid for my train ticket down to Edinburgh, to attend the funeral — I being broke! I stayed with my dear friend Heather, who had to put up with a great deal... I had severe short term memory loss (highly embarrassing!), an uncontrollable twitch in my left arm (even more embarrassing!), and to top it all, I caught a stomach bug, that even two bottles of 'kaolin and morphine' couldn't help!

Always a strong stubborn sort of a person, I was infuriated by this enormous array of ailments, especially the twitching arm. Every so often, it would jerk, and I'd scan the room, terrified someone had noticed!

But being amongst friends was a soothing balm, they were sympathetic, kindly, and helped me to laugh again. By the day of the funeral, though still racked by stomach pains, I was strong. Heather came with me to Mortonhall Crematorium, and so did Mum and Sheena. I was confident that I would be able to act an 'in control' part.

But I was poll-axed, when I saw the coffin arrive. To my shame all the control vanished, and I wept afresh. It was a quiet ceremony with friends, relatives, and performers that Dad had known, all there. Dad's wonderful *The Long Journey South* 'Whale music' was heard again, and now, for me it will always be a hauntingly sad, but beautiful sound.

After the service was over, there was a reception at the Braid Hills Hotel. This was slightly easier to handle. I talked with many people who had known Dad. People from the BBC, other musicians and performers, and many of his old friends. Grown-up children from my own childhood, echoed astonishment at how we had all changed, and it was a fine chance to swop news. Grandad, as down to earth as always, added a slight hint of humour to the sad day, by polishing off a huge silver salver of dainty sandwiches, and then rabbit-like, munching a fistful of parsley decoration. Later I caught him trapping some BBC people in a corner, and enthusiastically singing his favourite rendition of *The Flower of Scotland* in a wide range of tones — helped enormously by the many pints of beer!

Good old Grandad, I loved him for his friendly down to earth personality, he could take on the world and charm it.

Heather and I collected all the flowers from the crematorium, and with the car filled to overflowing with fresh bouquets carrying Dad's name. We took them to a nearby children's hospital, where the magnificent displays would brighten and cheer the patients there. Dad would have wanted that.

I suppose, if I could have chosen the ideal funeral service for Dad, and anything had been possible, I would have chosen the Vikings' way. The dead Viking warrior was laid on his longship and cast adrift out to sea, and the vessel set alight. A splendid send-off indeed, that would have linked Dad's Viking origins with his love of the sea. Just as they celebrate in Shetland with Up Helly-Ya.

They say it takes two years to get over the death of someone close.

I don't think I will truly ever get over Dad's loss, but I do think a little of the side effects of the trauma disappears after two years.

27

From the moment of Dad's death, and for about twenty-four months afterwards, unbidden and unannounced, I heard constantly in my mind, The Corries singing their songs on stage.

I was not going crazy. I could function as normal, and carry on my work and with other pastimes. But incessantly playing through my mind was every song The Corries had ever sung. It wasn't just Dad's songs, Ronnie's solos were there too. I could hear every harmony, every instrumental guitar piece, with amazing clarity. I could have understood it if it was only Dad I heard, and if it was only snatches of half-remembered songs. But as though I had a personal stereo inbuilt behind my ears, I could hear whole performances! There were songs played that normally I couldn't even have hummed let alone repeat, lyrics I'd heard perhaps once only.

It's a strange thing the subconscious. Obviously the hidden depths of my mind had 'taped' every Corrie performance, and now triggered by deep loss, they playing it back to me. I carried on at work as normal, instructing and conversing with people as normal, while in the background, heard only by me, beautiful renditions of *The Loch Tay Boat Song, Dark Lochnagar, The Hills of Ardmorn,* or the jaunty cheery strains of *The Portree Kid, The Rattlin' Bog,* and of course at other moments *The Flower of Scotland* complete with audience acclaim. Every song I'd ever heard, was available to me in its entirety, I don't think I played any of the selection of Corrie tapes that I had, I didn't need to!

The constant concerts are gone now, and I am back to my normal state of hearing snatches of this or that, and half remembered verses, which is reassuring, and at least makes listening to the tapes more viable again!

photo: Bill Robertson

Both Dad and Ronnie won a Gold Disc for their popularity with one of their compilation CDs. Dad's was awarded after his death, but I knew he would have been really chuffed indeed, and who knows perhaps he knows all about it! After all, Ronnie himself said Dad would be carrying on the music 'Up on High' — only it would be him teaching the angels!

I asked my sister Sheena if she would like to share some of her own memories of our father in these pages, and she sent me the following:

> My father took great delight in and was a connoisseur of the incongruous. He had an affection behind his humour which smiled at some of the ridiculous things out of which other people make a lot of sense. He rarely simply gave advice, rather he'd select a joke about the situation and let the joke itself impart the advice to the listening person.

He was fascinating company. He spoke slowly and softly as if measuring out the depth and dimensions of the words he chose, to see if he could create more of them later.

Relaxed and always finding something to be impressed about... or moved by... he liked to share his interests and the way he 'shared' made one feel chosen specially. He could talk someone over to his own point of view but do it in such a charmed way that the other person would feel it was a universally-held logical point of view.

He seemed to have an inbuilt Devil's advocate whom he continually consulted. In this regard he could sympathize with his opponents in a quarrel. In fact I'd go as far as saying he could 'see' from one extreme to the other of philosophies. He had, therefore, panoramic understanding.

Though his vision was panoramic, his tolerance was not always, and some of the time his irritable crankiness imbued those in his company with a sense of being an inconvenience.

He seemed to be in a different time-zone to everyone else, he even walked with a certain gracefulness in his stride that seemed to have an entirely different gravity to that of others.

Most folk would scurry, chicken-like, across a busy road where cars seem to dash in all directions. My father waded across such a road. In fact my father waded his way through life as though it were a heavy dark river he'd been through a thousand times before.

He had a great affection for innocence that was not patronizing or overly sentimental. He genuinely related well to animals and children and had an almost nostalgic respect for the wisdom of both.

Dad yawned and sneezed louder than anyone I've ever known, yet he ate his food so politely and discreetly that it was a surprise to find his plate clear at the end of a meal because somehow he could talk and eat at the same time without our being aware of him having done so.

He held his musical instruments like babies (having special telepathic relationships with each of them) and he held babies like musical instruments, I discovered, after I'd had my baby and my father came to visit him. My baby, not yet one week old, yawned enormously, smacked his lips then began to doze off in my fathers arms, so my father began to talk 'Norwegian' to this, my puzzled little baby, who laughed when my father laughed in his most treacle-ish audience-pandering show biz style.

Dad was the only person I know who could do voice-over narratives of the sort of internal dialogue he thought animals or people were having to themselves in a manner of comedy that still left their integrity intact. He really did invite one to see the world through his eyes, his respect, his humour etc., and it was a nicer world for these glimpses of appreciation.

The world is a much too serious and grey a place without him. I miss him more than the feeling of 'missing' can miss.

He was a man apart.

Sheena and Roy

I went back to work.

The sun shone outside, and the tourists kept my mind going with all sorts of different questions. Life would never be the same again, but normality was returning.

I was still ill with my upset stomach, and had lost half a stone in one week, but decided to go ahead with a Long-Distance Ride I had entered months before. It was the Home International, and even the World Champion Endurance Rider from the United States would be there. I had told Dad all about it, and he'd been very enthusiastic about the event. Of course just being a beginner at this sport, I was doing the smallest mileage, some were riding 100 miles.

But weak, and light headed I still felt the old thrill of the challenge, and was proud Dad had known I'd be there. It was almost as if he'd cheated death, by us both being aware of this day of the competition.

The old mare and I rocketed through the finish, well within time, and received our award.

Life is full of ups and downs, and more sad news occurred some weeks later, when my little dog Corrie, who had been struggling with massive cancerous tumours, could take no more.

I was devastated by her death. She'd been all through the good and bad times, with me, and had become almost part of me. Dad had always laughed at her daft tricks, and suddenly that link with him was gone for good as well. The world was terribly big, and empty, without her boisterous, cheerful character. Surely there could be no more bad luck?

Surely now things would get better?

In a way they did. Mum, Sheena, and I became a family unit again, even though we lived miles apart. Dad is part of me too. I am intensely proud to be his daughter, and to know he lives on in me, and Sheena.

It was touching to find he had kept all the letters I'd ever written to him, since early childhood, also my report cards, and exam results from school. Unobtrusively, he'd been closer than I'd ever imagined...

Flashes of vivid childhood memories swept into my mind.

Dad shaving, in the bathroom of our house at Stirling Road, Edinburgh. I was about four or five years of age at that time. I wandered in. Staring in morbid fascination I watched him finish, then apply 'Brylcreem' to his hair.

"What's that, Daddy?"

"Brylcreem".

"Oh!" (no wiser.)

Silence then...for a while!

"Daddy, can I have Brylcreem on *my* hair?"

"NO!"

"Ooh, why not?"

"Well, girls are not supposed to wear Brylcreem!"

"Why not?"

Silence while he desperately thought about it.

"Can I Daddy, please? Oh, go on Daddy, *pleeeze?*"

Mum was horrified, when I wandered through, a proud look on my face, my blonde hair plastered to my skull in greasy, great streaks. "Look Mummy, just like Daddy now!"

"Oh *Roy!*" was all she could say, I felt very disappointed!

On long sleepless nights, when my legs had agonising cramp, Dad would get up about 3 a.m., stand me on the wooden kitchen table, and try and rub the circulation back into my tiny legs, even though he himself was exhausted. I think it was then that I solemnly told him, that when I grew up I was going to marry him!

On a couple of occasions he took me down to his pottery studios, by then in Henderson Row. I was fascinated how he worked the potter's wheel, and wheedled at him constantly, to let me have a shot. He allowed me to draw on one of the pots he'd made. I remember it so clearly.

Using a matchstick, under his careful guidance of not drawing too heavily, I drew the donkey carrying 'Mary and Joseph'. I can't remember why. (Probably it was a good excuse to draw something remotely connected with horses.) Anyway Dad liked it for its primitive style, even if I had to explain which of the three figures was the donkey!

I have that pot to this day, it haunts me a welcome happy memory.

When we were a little older, just a little, for a treat, Dad would take us to Crawfords Restaurant, just down from George Street. The biggest goldfish in the whole wide world, swam in an inside pond there. Dad would give us pennies to drop in, and we'd all make a wish. I could almost swear, that my little sister used to fire her pennies with frighteningly deadly aim at the poor fish! But then she never did like uneventful occasions!

Much later in life, when Dad had the *Sheena Margaret* moored at Granton Harbour, he liked to have a 'one of the boys' image, meaning by that, that he dressed, spoke, and acted, like one of the fishing boat crews. And on pain of death...I was not to appear down at the harbour in my riding jodhpurs, it would have made him look too 'Yuppie'! He used to get terribly irate at the rich sailing people who took it for granted that they could make fast their expensive yachts alongside his fishing boat, the *Sheena Margaret*! He used to curse about that for hours, plotting all kinds of horrible revenges, which he had always forgotten about by the next visit to his boat... thank goodness!

Even towards the end of his life, he'd sometimes turn up at one of my horse shows, to watch me compete. The last time was when I was riding someone else's stallion, luckily we did quite well that day and I didn't let him down. It meant an awful lot, my Dad coming to watch, especially as he tended to dislike the stereotyped 'Huntin, Fishin, Shootin' people he thought he was bound to meet there, and he always felt trapped by his fame and the fear he might be recognised by one of them. But to me it was like the sun shining to see him there.

28

We scattered Dad's ashes on the sea off Hopeman, and in the little rockpools along the shore there, the remainder were cast in the grounds at Gordonstoun school, and some under his favourite tree, a weeping birch.

Actually, Dad had the last laugh there. We were so busy, ordering each other about, as to the best way to plant the tree, that by the time we had finished and stood back to admire the tree, I realised with dawning horror that we'd forgotten to plant Dad's ashes under it! He'd really have chuckled at that.

One of the nicest images I have of that day, is one of little David (my sister's son, and Dad's only grandson, then aged four), standing at the edge of the sea wearing, like a huge dress, Dad's favourite jumper. I suppose David did not entirely understand why we were scattering his grandfather's ashes, and it was refreshing to all of us to see him treat the whole excursion as one whopper of an adventure. But as David stood at the water's edge, willing the waves to go away, it seemed to me that the line goes on, that Death can't steal it all...that in me, Sheena, and now David, Dad lives on.

Some months later, I cycled to his house in Forres for Christmas. I was alone, the rest of the family were miles away in Edinburgh, or seeking the comfort of other relatives.

It was a cold Christmas Day, the streets of Forres were deserted. But I was keeping a promise. The promise I'd made to Dad before he died.

"If times get tough, think of Christmas," I had said. I was going to spend a few minutes of Christmas in the room where he died. The house was quiet. The lights cast a soft, dim, glow, and I sat down on the sofa, and looked all around at the physical things that had been his. My memory flickered back, over happier times, and then over all the Christmases I could remember.

Leaning slightly forwards, I covered my face with my hands, so as not to be distracted by my surroundings, and sent a prayer to Dad. Then I repeated, "I love you always, Dad. Think of Christmas at the cottage."

In the blackness of my shielded sight, for a brief second, I saw a strange pattern of pinprick size lights. There were four, in a rough square shape, with a further scattering in a tail

(above): on the sea off Hopeman... me, my nephew David, and my sister
(left): ...the little rock-pools along the shore (my mother, David and me)

attached. "Funny," I thought, blinking my eyes open, I put it down to the pressure of my hands against my eyes.

Cycling home again, was much easier than coming in. I had been frightened, I think, of not being able to handle my grief, but now I felt peaceful. I had kept my promise to be with Dad at Christmas.

I suppose it's difficult for bereaved people to come to terms with the undeniable fact that someone has gone for good. They tend to look for signs in everything. All of us close to him did the same. But I was absolutely dumbfounded when I went out to feed the horse late that night.

The stars were out, and sparkling in the frosty, black, night air, and there, above my head, with glittering purity, shone the exact same pattern that I'd seen in my hands at Forres.

"*It's Dad's stars, Dad's stars!*" I told the old mare, as she crunched rhythmically at her hay. He had always gone for a walk with me in the winter nights, and especially at Christmas, to talk about the stars. I remembered it all now. Later, I looked up in a book, and found that the pattern was known as the Plough. But that particular night, I stood staring upwards at the vastness of the sky, knowing that Dad had *not* gone, just *changed.*

Nothing is gone for good. Atoms can be rearranged, particles shifted, but not destroyed completely. Dad would always be there, in the gentle breeze, or howling gale, the storm tossed waves, or lyrical rivers. There, too, in the pleasure of the Autumn trees, and in the immortal stars. And always, ever always in his songs, and the memories of us all...

"*...He's no awa', tae bide awa...*"

2 9

In 1992, I was invited to the official opening of The Corries exhibition in memory of my father, held in Forres museum.

I declined.

I was frightened that I would not be able to control my emotions at seeing my father's musical instruments, sealed up, out of context, and silent for ever. I was also frightened of making a fool of myself, by bursting into tears, in front of the local Forres dignitaries! It went against the 'Williamson' grain, baring my feelings in public.

I was wrong.

My friend Mhari Ross understood my trepidation all too well, she remembered the loss of one of her own parents and could sympathise. I was a little curious about the display at the museum, and she arranged for me to have a private viewing in the early evening after the public had gone.

The museum itself is not very big, and it was a bit strange, to walk in to the place devoid of bustling tourists. As we

the TV series "The Corries and Other Folk" won an International Gold Medal in 1983 passed all the historic relics of the past, I thought how Dad would have loved to study the fossils and rocks, pictish weapons, and implements of long ago though he would have avoided the museum like the plague whilst open to the public, being at heart reclusive and shy.

Mhari and the museum representative were terrific, putting me at my ease. The Corrie exhibition was not large, and yet it dominated quite a proportion of the building. Myself, relatives, and Ronnie Browne, had donated a few items; a few others were obtained by the Museum itself. I do think it needs more, and if any of the fans or friends would like to loan, or give, items, I believe the Museum and all its visitors would be very grateful.

On the walls were sleeves from different albums, posters from different tours, going away back in time. In a glass case, hung one of Dad's older handmade guitars, a flute, a tin penny whistle, a mouth organ, and with a sharp pang of grief I recognised a concertina, complete with its carrying box. Unbidden and unrestricted, memories flashed into my

photos: Norman Wilson

mind... Dad sitting in front of the fire, jauntily creating new sea-shanties with the concertina, his fingers dancing over the ivory buttons, his head half tilted in concentration but eyes alight with good humour. Other images of the times he'd played it alongside my grandfather's accordion, in an impromptu concert, the rest of us joining in with singing, or playing the spoons. The concertina now sat silent, no longer needed by its owner. The reasoning part of me could understand the joy its presence would bring to pilgriming fans. They did not have the same memories I had, and it was important that these instruments, if they could not be played again, should, at least, be seen, rather than forgotten on some shelf.

Newspaper cuttings, a brief history of The Corries, and mention of some of Dad's hobbies festooned another wall. But best of all were the ongoing videos. My emotions turned to happiness, as a collection of The Corries songs were performed on the screens. Pride soared within my flagging soul, as the giant army of rugby supporters, at the Grand Slam in Murrayfield, sang with all their patriotic energy, Dad's song. Even better, after the songs, a second video, taken from a documentary on The Corries, some years ago, depicted Dad and Ronnie in happy banter with the interviewer, whilst rehearsing informally at home. I remembered the film being recorded, but till now had forgotten all about it. Suddenly there in front of me, Dad, my scruffy homely Dad, was chatting away, and moving around, very much alive. I smiled at his long sideburns, height of fashion then, noticing too how dark Ronnie's hair was in those days.

I approved wholeheartedly of the exhibition, and thought that it was good that the visitors would be able to see this last video-recording, which was unobtainable anywhere else, and yet brought out the natural side of Dad's character.

I thanked the Museum representative, and walked with Mhari out into the chilly evening sunshine. The apprehension with which I had approached the building was now replaced by a sense of peace.

I do not have very much Corrie memorabilia.

But on reaching home I searched quickly through what I did have, that might be of use. I unearthed a few photographs, some letters and postcards, a few old programmes, which Mhari passed on to the museum.

I'd like to go back again.

This time I will go in opening hours, knowing I can control the sharp spontaneity of grief, and have the confidence that in the crowd no one will notice anyway!

Dad lived and died in Forres.

It's fitting his memory lives on here.

Remembered with pride, by his local folk.